THE
FAIR WEATHER AND RAINY DAY
HANDY BOOK

THE
FAIR
WEATHER AND
RAINY DAY
HANDY
BOOK

Daniel C. Beard

Dover Publications, Inc.
Mineola, New York

Bibliographical Note

This Dover edition, first published in 2009, is an unabridged republication of the 1921 printing of the work originally published by Charles Scribner's Sons, New York, in 1900 under the title *New Ideas for American Boys: The Jack of All Trades*.

Library of Congress Cataloging-in-Publication Data

Beard, Daniel Carter, 1850–1941.
    The fair weather and rainy day handy book / Daniel C. Beard. — Dover ed.
      p. cm.
    Originally published: New ideas for American boys. New York : C. Scribner's sons, 1900.
    Includes index.
    ISBN-13: 978-0-486-47403-8
    ISBN-10: 0-486-47403-8
    1. Amusements. 2. Sports. I. Beard, Daniel Carter, 1850–1941. New ideas for American boys. II. Title.

TT160.B359 2009
796—dc22

                                          2009018986

Manufactured in the United States by Courier Corporation
47403801
www.doverpublications.com

PREFACE

IT was not the author's original intention to produce a series of boys' books. On the contrary, he expected that his work in this line would begin and end with "The American Boy's Handy Book."

The great popularity of that book is a constant source of gratification and pleasure to the author ; but he was not a little surprised and embarrassed when he discovered that in place of satisfying the lads he had only whetted their appetite for more material in the same line. Letters from boys in many parts of the British Provinces, and from all over the United States, convinced the writer that he had yet work to do for them, and the revised and enlarged edition of "The American Boy's Handy Book" was issued. After a brief period of time the quaintly worded letters in boyish handwriting began again to increase the mail left at the author's studio, and this time he laid aside his brush and pencil to produce "The Outdoor Handy Book."

It is hoped that the present demand for new ideas for boys will be fully satisfied by "The Jack of All Trades." To the best of the author's knowledge and belief there is not a thing described in this book which has not been proved practical by the experiments of himself or some boy or boys. Parts of this book have appeared in various periodicals, but all these chapters have been revised and enlarged.

It is now a generally accepted truth that the so-called skill of the hand is in reality the skill of a trained mind. The necessity, in work or play, of constantly overcoming new obstacles and solving new problems, develops a strong and normal mind and body. There can be little doubt that the rude schooling and hard knocks of a pioneer's life rejuvenated our race and developed those qualities in the characters of Americans, without which Washington would have been but a country gentleman and Lincoln a village store-keeper. Had little Abe Lincoln been reared under the care of a foreign woman with cap and ribbons (*i.e.* a French nurse), his strong manly character would never have been developed and our country would have lost one of its grandest patriots and history its most unique figure.

Aside from these vitally important facts, art demands that our youth should be encouraged to do things for themselves, to produce things by their own labor. The most finished product of the machine cannot appeal to the heart of a real artist as does some useful and homely object which still bears the marks of its maker's hands.

For these reasons the author hopes that parents will allow their boys to be boyish boys; and in order to keep them out of mischief they will cater to the lads' natural and healthy desire for entertainment by encouraging them in all rational projects and supplying them with tools and materials, so that the boys may all become juvenile Jacks of All Trades.

It is the object of the author, in the chapters devoted to animal life, to teach the boys to look upon all animals with the same thoughtful kindness with which they might view their own undeveloped brothers.

To Harper & Brothers, and to *The Ladies' Home Journal* the thanks of the author are due for the careful preservation and return of such original drawings as were used by them in their respective publications, and without which this work would be incomplete.

D. C. B.

FLUSHING, June 1, 1900.

CONTENTS.

PART I.

FAIR WEATHER IDEAS.

CHAPTER I.

CHAPTER II.

CHAPTER III.

CHAPTER XIII.

CHAPTER XIV.

CHAPTER XV.

PART II.

RAINY DAY IDEAS.

CHAPTER XVI.

CHAPTER XVII.

PART I.

FAIR WEATHER IDEAS.

CHAPTER I.

TREE-TOP CLUB HOUSES.

It is now over thirty years since the writer was first initiated into the delights of a boys' club-house in the tree-tops, and it happened in this way:

The war of the Rebellion was over; for four years the fathers, big brothers, teachers, and policemen of the border States had had so much serious fighting on their own hands that little or no attention was paid to the growing generation of boys, and they were left to fight their own battles in their own way.

For four eventful years these boys were under practically no other restraint than the little their poor half-distracted mothers could enforce. The boys, however, did not appear to miss the discipline, nor desire it, and, as far as their physical health was concerned, they throve and developed into lusty lads, though many of them recognized no law but that of physical force.

Gangs of young toughs, under the leadership of local bullies, frequented the play-grounds and roamed along the river-fronts, where they hunted down, pillaged, and beat every unprotected lad they could catch out of sight of his own home.

3

In spite of the fact that the river-fronts were the favorite resorts of the lawless element, those places presented so many attractions to the juvenile mind that they were the popular play-grounds of all the boys living within reach of their muddy banks and turbid waters.

About this time three boys of a Kentucky town, who were devoted to boating and bathing, put their curly heads together to devise a plan by which they might enjoy their favorite pastimes, and at the same time secure a safe place of refuge where they could hide when the enemy approached in numbers too strong for the three boys to resist.

After many conferences, and references to " Robinson Crusoe," " Swiss Family Robinson," " The Coral Islands," and other undoubted authorities, they decided to build an underground house,* and armed with spades and shovels, they immediately began work right in the heart of the enemy's country.

They worked, as only boys can when they think their work is fun, and soon excavated a great hole in the river-bank.   Not far off were the remains of a flat-boat, and to the heavy pieces of timber the boys harnessed themselves and hauled the lumber over the top of their cave to serve for a roof.

With spade and shovel they carefully concealed the timber by a thick layer of earth, leaving only a square hole with a trap-door as an entrance and exit.   The dirt was then smoothed down, and drift-wood, dried weeds, and other rubbish scattered over in such a manner that no one, without careful inspection, would suspect that the bank had been tampered with.

But the enemy was alert, and spies had been stealthily

---

* Chapter VIII. of this book tells how to build an underground club-house.

watching the work progress, and patiently waiting the completion of the secret hiding-place. No sooner was the last handful of rubbish strewn over the roof than, with wild yells and whoops of delight, the "River Rats" charged upon the surprised workers.

"Big Red" Resmere in the lead, with "Squinty" Quinn and "Spotty," the freckled-face, close behind, while the rear was brought up with a rabble of less noted characters, who more than made up for their own lack of courage by their terror-inspiring yells. It was too formidable a crowd for the three cave-diggers to parley with, so they ingloriously fled up the bank, leaving the product of their hard work in the hands of the despoilers.

The River Rats

used the cave as headquarters, and for a long time afterward would suddenly sally forth from the concealment of the hole and surprise and beat any strange lad who was incautious enough to venture in the neighborhood unprotected by a company of friends. This adventure taught us several things, and one night, at the "dark of the moon," we met in a smoke-house and formed ourselves into a secret society. Over a bottle of strained honey we made solemn vows, and the secrets of the society have never been divulged until now.

The name, the purpose, and the fact of there being any society were the three great secrets. The name was "The Three Ancient Mariners." The object was to stand by each other to the crack of doom, and the seal, 3·A·M, was tattooed on each member's good right arm.

The vows were religiously kept, and many a bruised face and discolored eye proved our loyalty to each other, for the River Rats made constant war upon us, and our

peaceful plans for fun were often rudely upset by the sudden appearance of a bright red head, followed by a freckled
face and a gang of retainers.

This persecution caused the production of

A Tree-top Retreat,

which, I believe, has never yet been discovered by the
enemy, nor any one else.*   To reach our secret camp and
club-house we had to trudge along the dusty turnpike in
the hot sun, with no shade but that afforded by our wide-
brimmed straw hats.   After passing an old-fashioned inn,
with its swinging sign decorated with a picture of the battle of Buena Vista, we cut cross-lots over the forts and
rifle-pits on the hill-side, built by the Union soldiers at the
time of the Morgan raid.   At the end of the lowest rifle-pit
we slid down the cut to the railroad track, and followed it
to the fence, with a hollow gate-post, where the bluebirds
always built their nests.   Here we left the railway and en-
tered a cool belt of woods in which the dainty maidenhair-
ferns grew on the damp rotten logs and the gray squirrels
scolded us from the branches overhead.   Following a private
trail, we reached an immense beech-tree which had grown
around a shaggy-barked hickory in such a manner that only
the roots and branches of the hickory could be seen, the
whole trunk being embedded and concealed by the smooth
bark of the beech, giving it the novel appearance of a tree
bearing two entirely different kinds of nuts.

Under the spreading branches of this compound tree
we generally rested awhile and took a look about us, to be
certain that the River Rats were not on our trail ; then

---

* Since the above was written the writer visited the place, found the woods gone
and trolley cars running by the old camp.

diving into the hazel thicket, we emerged on the banks of a tributary to the Licking River. A giant tulip-tree stood on the bank of the creek, and a wild grape-vine, as thick as your arm, dangled from the branches, which spread like an umbrella sixty or seventy feet above us. The vine had been cut loose from its roots on the shore, and its severed end hung over a deep, dark pool.

The Secret Grape-Vine Route.

No boy, outside the members of the 3·A·M's, would look twice at the great snake-like vine hanging over the "lick," and if he should, the vine was far out of reach, and would be passed by as suggesting no possibilities of fun.

Well, that is where he would make his mistake. Concealed in the underwood back of the tulip-tree was a long pole with a hook on one end, and by means of this imple-

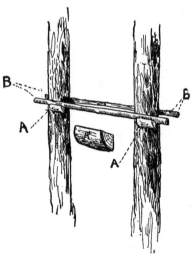

FIG. 1.—Beginning a Two-tree Foundation.

ment we could grapple the grape-vine and pull the end within reach of our hands, and then one of us at a time would grasp the vine securely with both hands, and stepping back on the bank, give a short run, spring out into mid-air and sail away across the deep hole to drop with a thud upon the opposite bank.

Of course all this was unnecessary, for there were plenty of shallow riffs near by where we could wade across; but no lad with any romance in his soul would be guilty of such baby-work when he knew the secret of the grape-vine route.

Once across we would peer carefully around in the most approved Indian-scout fashion, and when satisfied the coast was clear we would crouch down and make a wide detour that would bring us to a large sycamore-tree, which had been uprooted by the wind and fallen so that its top rested in the fork of a towering oak-tree. The spreading roots of the fallen sycamore made a wall of clay fully fifteen feet high, which, with the surrounding underbrush and foliage, effectually concealed the fact that in the branches of the oak-tree rested a large and strange nest—a nest built by wingless birds, for it was the club-house of the Three Ancient Mariners! The leaning trunk of the uprooted tree made a firm though slippery substitute for a ladder, and here among the branches many a jolly day was passed, and many a meal of fried fish, fresh from the neighboring "lick," was devoured by three happy, sunburned boys.

Dangerous Toughs.

Except in the neighborhood of large cities, there is nowadays not much danger from gangs of brutal, half-grown boys, but in those times the law seldom bothered any one.

However, even now, privacy and exemption from unwelcome interruption are desirable, and this can be best secured by

A Club-House in the Tree-tops,

for when the ladder is pulled up no one, without the aid of "climbers," such as line-men use, can hope to gain access to the cosey little house in the branches.

If you can find a tree with three or four strong spreading

Tree-top House.

6 x 10 feet, 35 feet from ground to floor.

branches, the problem of erecting a house is not a difficult one. If there are four straight trees the proper distance apart, it is a comparatively simple work to erect your house between their trunks, high enough to be out of reach of River Rats; but trees, as a rule, do not regulate their growth to suit any set of boys, and the boys must use their ingenuity to adapt their houses to the forms and growth of the available trees.

First choose your location, and see that it is a desirable one to all the club members; then, if there are any lofty trees at

The Desired Spot

you will certainly find an opportunity for a four-tree, three-tree, two-tree, or one-tree house.

The tree or trees for the purpose must be so tall, that when the bottom ladder is pulled up the house will be out of reach of unwelcome callers, and big enough to prevent the wind from so swaying the house as to give a feeling of insecurity.

A Two-Tree House.

Let us suppose that there are only two trees in the proper location which fulfil the requirements, and that these are tall pines with no branches of any importance below their feather-duster-like tops. This presents one of the most difficult problems to solve; but when you know how, you can erect a most enchanting "crow's-nest" away up the tall trunks, where the fresh breeze blows over the tops of the smaller trees, and where a good view can be had of the surrounding country, and the enemy, if there be one, may be seen while yet a long distance off, giving ample time to the club members to pull up the ground ladder and place themselves in position to laugh at the foe.

How To Start.

With an accomplished woodsman the whole edifice may be erected with the use of no other tool than an axe; but, as a rule, the more tools you have at your disposal the better you can do your work. If you possess a tape-line, measure the distance with it between the two tree-trunks. If you have no tape but have a two-foot ruler, make yourself a

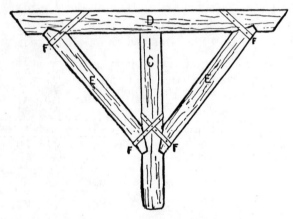

FIG. 2.—King Posts and Corbel.

longer measure by marking off the feet and half-feet upon a ten or twelve-foot pole, and use it to measure between the trees. If, however, you have neither, use your legs and pace the distance, and then cut two long, strong poles, and see that they are long enough to span the distance between the trees, leaving plenty of wood to project beyond each tree. Flatten one side of each pole as shown in the diagram B, B, Fig. 1. Next, select a sound log, a foot or so in diameter, quarter it, and make four

A Blocks,

each about two feet long. See A, A,
and A¹, Fig 1.

As it is best to have the bottom of
your house level, you must manage to
nail the A blocks the same distance
above the ground on each side of each
tree—that is, if the ground is level; if
not, you must allow for the slant of the
earth. Spike the blocks securely to the
trees with six-inch nails, using about
three nails to each block.

The foundation of the house may be
higher than your ladder will reach. In
this case cut two more poles
and four more blocks, and
at the point where the top
of your ladder reaches spike
on the blocks, and then rest

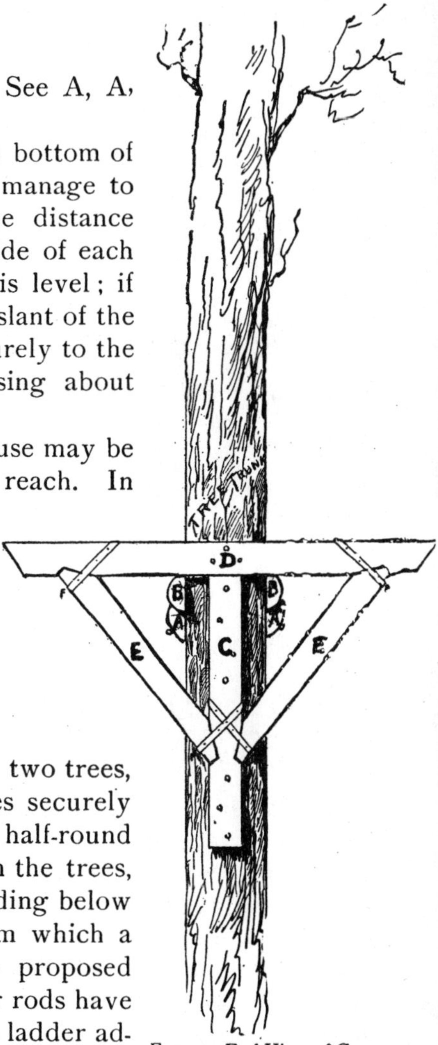

The B Poles

on them on each side of the two trees,
as in Fig 1. Nail the B poles securely
to the tree, and with plank or half-round
sticks floor the space between the trees,
and you will have a good landing below
your house (see Fig. 5) from which a
ladder may be run to the proposed
foundation. After the upper rods have
been nailed to the trees and a ladder ad-
justed, and for security nailed fast to

FIG. 3.—End View of Cor-
bel Resting on B Sticks.

the tree and lower platform, you are ready to begin the
serious work of building.   Take a good strong plank, two
inches thick, and cut two pieces about six feet long, and
shaped as shown by

The Corbel Piece D

in Fig. 2 ; then cut four struts (E, E, in Fig. 2) and two
king-posts (C, Fig 2).   Shave off the ends of the struts, as

FIG. 4.—Perspective View of Corbels Resting on B Sticks.

shown in the diagram, to fit the notches cut in the corbel
pieces and the king-posts.

It is not necessary to spike this frame together—the
big nails might split the timber—they may be fastened together slightly with wire nails and strengthened by a piece
of hoop-iron nailed on with small nails, as shown in Fig 2

FIG. 5.—A Two-Tree House.

at F, F, F, F, and this will keep the pieces from accidentally slipping out of their bearings, or holes may be bored and the parts held together with screws. The real strain being an up-and-down thrust on the notches, the weight will not bear upon the iron bands or screws. Great care must be taken to make neat-fitting joints.

How to Build the Foundation.

When the two pieces of the form of Fig. 2 are completed, make fast a line to them and haul them up the tree ; then slip the ends of the rods B and B under the corbels D, until the king-post C lies flat against the side of the tree-trunk. Spike C securely to the tree-trunk, as shown in Fig. 3 ; do the same with the other frame on the far side of the other tree, and you have a firm foundation that will hold more weight than you are liable to put upon it. Now cut two more pieces of two-inch plank, say, ten feet long by four inches broad ; hoist them up and spike them to the top of the corbel pieces D, D, so that they will project the same distance beyond the tree at each end, as in Fig. 4.

From G to G you may now lay the planks of your floor, if the distance is short : if not, put two poles across each side of the trees and nail them to the trunks, and two more across at each end of the pieces G, G, and nail them to G and G, and then put your flooring on parallel to the G planks.

Frame, Walls, and Roof.

The rest of the work is simple. To shed the rain your roof must incline one way or the other—to the front, as in Fig. 5, or to the back, as in the one-tree house, Fig. 6. Nail on an A block to each tree, and give them the same incline ; then place two poles for rafters on the A blocks,

FIG. 6.—Frame of a One-Tree House.

and nail them, each with a single nail, to the tree-trunk;
this will hold them in place until you cut four straight
poles for the uprights at the four corners of your house;
set these up under the ends of the rafters, and nail the

rafter to them and to the trees ; then drive two or three nails, slantingly, in the foot of the upright to secure them to the floor (toe-nail, Fig. 92, Chap. IX.). A cross-piece on top of the front and rear completes the skeleton of your house, which may be roofed and the sides covered with boards, or only the roof made of boards with narrow strips over the cracks and the sides covered with poles, by nailing the latter to the uprights as in Fig. 5. This gives a fine rustic effect, but unless ceiled or boarded up on the inside it will allow the wind and rain to beat through.

If the trees are further apart than desirable, the house can be built between the trees, as in Fig. 5, but if the space is no more than required, the house can be built so that the sides enclose the tree-trunks, as the railing of the platform does in Fig. 5.

A Rustic House.

It is really not necessary to use any plank or boards except for the roof and floor. A boy who can handle an axe and hatchet well can make the frame, Fig. 2, from timber cut in the woods, but unless he is an expert, or can get the services of an expert axeman, he had better use plank as directed.

The One-Tree House

at first thought seems to be an even more serious problem than the two-tree house, but a glance at Fig. 6 will show how it can be built without much trouble.

First we nail the two A blocks on to the trunk, then the two B sticks. After the two B sticks are placed upon the A blocks and nailed to the tree, two more B poles must be laid over the first at right angles to them, so as to enclose the tree-trunk within a square of B sticks. Nail all four sticks securely to the tree. You will notice that in this case many of the sticks are notched near the ends, as D is in Fig. 2, and for a similar purpose, to receive and hold the ends of the struts, which are nailed at their lower ends to the king-post (trunk of the tree). It is unnecessary to notch or mar the trunk of the tree, for the ends of the struts are cut on an angle to rest flat against the trunk where they are nailed, and the nails will not injure the tree in the least.

Fig. 6 shows the roof boards laid clinker, or lap-streak fashion, from side to side. Where a roof is laid in this manner it is not necessary or desirable to nail strips over the cracks, as these are fully protected by the overlapping boards.

FIG. 7.—Three-Tree House.

Wherever it seems necessary to add to the stability of the foundation of any of the club-houses described, it can be done by struts from the tree-trunk to the ends of the B sticks or other poles supporting the structure.

Figs. 7 and 8 show, respectively,

A Three- and Four-Tree Foundation,

equally applicable to a three or four branch foundation.
It is, of course, impossible for the writer to give exact
figures and iron-clad rules for this style of building, owing to the variable nature and growth of the trees, but the most difficult problems are here solved, and any other combination of trees or branches will be found to be only variations of the ones here illustrated and described.

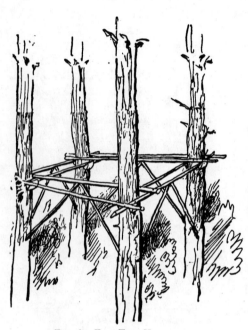

FIG. 8.—Four-Tree House.

As I remember our little house in the Kentucky oak-tree, it must have been but a rude affair, yet it was dearer to the hearts of the 3 · A · M's than a house and lot on Fifth Avenue would be now to the only living member of the club formed over thirty years ago.

CHAPTER II.

HUNTING WITHOUT A GUN.

How to Capture and Trap Small Live Animals.

A BOY who can spend part of his time out of town, and is the fortunate owner of a mongrel cur, forms a combination for enjoyment and fun hard to be beaten by anything in nature. A good yellow dog, unencumbered by any aristocratic ancestors, is an ideal companion in the wood, and field: it can scent a woodchuck leagues away, it knows just how to head a chipmonk off from its retreat, and there is not a trick known to the professional poacher which is not familiar to the real country plebeian cur. .

Chipmonks and Woodchucks!

There is a potent charm in those words, which can iron the wrinkles out of an old brow, and soften the hard lines in the face of a careworn professional or business man.

Not long ago I attended a dinner given by the

Camp-Fire Club,

and there I found ranged around the table an array of veteran hunters. There were men there who had hunted the royal Bengal tiger in the jungles of India, men who had fought with rogue elephants, men who had followed the lions to their dens in Africa, men who had tracked the white

bear to its lair in the far frozen North. There were gentlemen who hunted for pleasure, cowboys and scouts—Co-
quina Shields, " Wolf " Thompson, " Curio " Brown, "Yel-
lowstone" Kelly, Andrew J. Stone, and many others equally
well-known in the forests or on the plains were seated at
the big round table.*

That they were real simon-pure sportsmen could be
seen at a glance, and yet, when the after-dinner speeches
were made, the sentiments which received the most enthusi-
astic applause were those which DENOUNCED THE KILLING
OF MAN OR BEAST. It could readily be seen that these men
only used the gun when it was necessary to procure food or
in self-defence. They all indorsed the use of the camera
for the hunt in place of the murderous gun ; as one of them
remarked, " With a kodak every good shot is registered
with the click of the shutter, and an album of good shots is
a thing of which any man may be proud."

With a little private zoo of captured live game you may
have a living album, which attests the skill of the collector
and his knowledge of woodcraft as accurately as any album
of photographs.

The next chapter tells how to build a back-yard zoo, and
now we must learn how to stock one. If the reader will

* G. O. Shields, President of the League of American Sportsmen, editor of
Recreation.

Ernest Seton-Thompson, naturalist to the Government of Manitoba, author of
" Wild Animals I Have Known."

Capt. Luther S. Kelly, veteran of the War of '61 and Spanish War, Indian
fighter, one of General Custer's scouts and hunters.

William Harvey Brown, African traveller, hunter and collector for the United
States Museum, author of " On the South African Frontier."

A. J. Stone, field naturalist, arctic explorer, hero of a 3,000-mile sledge journey,
discoverer of several American mammals new to science.

Making a Capture.

examine the plans in the chapter mentioned, he will see that there is one compartment marked

" Receiving-Cage."

This is the place where our new captures find temporary shelter until their regular quarters are prepared for them. The most accessible game for boys belongs to the

Rodents or Gnawers.

These animals can be readily distinguished by their long, chisel-like front teeth. A familiar example of this family may be found in every town and city, and is known as the common rat, the Norway rat, or the brown rat.

Formerly the common rat of the United States was black, but his brown relative has about exterminated the more graceful black one. The only black rat I ever saw was a dead one, which I found one summer in an unoccupied house in the mountains of Pennsylvania. But there are plenty of beautiful little gnawers around us everywhere. There are the soft, furry, big-eyed flying-squirrels, which leave their warm nests at dusk and sail through the air from tree to tree, or romp among the branches until daylight. Just at dawn they return to their beds, to sleep away the day in their dark holes, secure from the garish sunlight.

Of course any boy with money can purchase flying-squirrels, but no boy with any pride would stoop to buy his live game, unless he is so unfortunate as to be unable to leave the densely populated city. I well remember the two boys* who gave me my first lessons in hunting flying-squir-

---

* Charles Dana Gibson, the artist, and his brother, Langdon Gibson, naturalist and traveller.

rels.   I followed them across meadows, over hills, through
the woods, down into the dank and dark swamps, until we
found some old hollow cedars on the edge of the water.
Here one of the lads armed himself with a small wand, and
the other busied himself gathering old dry leaves and bits
of moist bark to make a smudge.   The boy armed with the
wand probed the hollow trees until he discovered a hole
from which the wand would bring forth some bits of the
fine shredded inner bark of the cedar.
We all know that neither the inner
bark nor any other
kind of bark grows
in the hollow of
trees, and when it is discovered there you can wager that
it was put there by some animal.

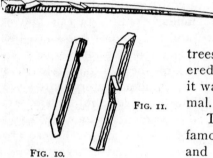

Fig. 9.

Fig. 11.

Fig. 10.

This stringy, soft stuff is
famous material for a nest,
and both the white-footed
mice and the flying-squirrels
are fully aware of its good properties.

When some of this nesting is found in a tree, it is safe
to say that there is a nest inside.

A Smudge

is now lighted and the hollow tree is filled with smoke. As
soon as this is thoroughly done, you may safely thrust your
arm into the hollow and bring out the stupefied inmates.

I never knew the smoke to cause the squirrels any serious harm.   The little captives soon revive, when brought
out into the open air.

Flying-Squirrels,

when tame, make the most gentle pets, but when wild, and rudely seized by hand, they have a vicious way of using their chisel-like teeth which induces more caution the next time. A smoke-stupefied squirrel is much more pleasant to handle than a wild one, frantic with fright.

If, however, you protect your hand with an ordinary bicycle or golf cap, you can seize almost any small animal with impunity. I caught nine flying-squirrels in one night, with no protection for my hand but an old cloth cap.

Do not try to throw the cap over the animal, or it will escape from beneath, but use the cap as a protection to your hand, then grasp the creature by a quick movement, closing your fingers tightly over its body, being careful not to squeeze hard enough to injure the terrified little squirrel. The advantage of this mode of capture is that, having the game in your hand, you can easily thrust it into the cloth bag you carry for that purpose.

The Cloth Bag

is a most convenient thing; it is easy to carry, allows plenty of air, and the little creatures never think of gnawing out while you carry them.

I have carried

Short-Tailed Meadow-Rats

and white-footed mice for miles, tied up in my handker-chief, and no attempt was made by my prisoners to use their teeth to assist them in escaping.

The gentle, graceful little jumping-mice, white-footed mice, short-tailed meadow-rats, and flying squirrels are all to be found inside the city limits of Greater New York, and some of their relatives are to be found in almost any rural place in this country. These interesting little creatures can be captured with ordinary box-traps, figure fours, or the square or round wire mouse-traps. The white-footed mice or deer-mice may be found in the abandoned nests of other rodents, in hollow logs, in old corn-stacks, in holes in the fence-rails, and under clods of old ploughed fields, or beneath brush-heaps in the fence corners.

In the late autumn, before the first snow comes, they have a very pretty way of

Utilizing Last Summer's Birds'-Nests

by filling them with the soft down from the cat-tails of a neighboring marsh, or with moss and wood fibres, thistle-down, or the silky feathers from the seed of the milk-weed. Like flying-squirrels, the little deer-mice bury themselves in the soft nests, and sleep away the day, emerging at night for food and exercise.

If the branch upon which the nest is located is but

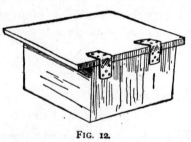

FIG. 12.

touched, the brown-backed, nimble-footed little squatter will poke his head from the middle of the nest, look inquiringly around, and if no danger appears the head is withdrawn, and the mouse resumes its slumbers; but if it is deemed that there is cause for serious alarm, it will spring from the nest, and with the agility of a squirrel run lightly up a branch, and from this point of vantage turn its bright eyes on the intruder with a sort of "please don't" expression. If further frightened it will hastily leap to the ground and disappear in the brush and dry leaves.

Sometimes I have found birds'-nests with a neatly laid thatch roof over the bowl, and a round doorway gnawed through the side of the nest for a means of access to the interior, where, snugly curled up in a warm bed of down, the little white-footed mouse was sleeping.

White-Footed Mice as Pets.

Once, while skating on a pond, I discovered a pair of deer-mice keeping house in the walls of the mound of mud and roots reared by musk-rats for their winter quarters.

FIG. 12A.—The Old Figure-Four Trap.—Any old box will do for a figure-four trap; but much trouble is avoided by using a box with a large lid for live game, as shown in Fig. 12. This is set upside down, as shown above. The lid is considerably larger than the box, and attached to it by a couple of leather hinges which are tacked to the lid and the box, as shown in the illustration. Fig. 9 is the spindle or trigger, and shows the manner in which the notches are cut. Fig. 10 is the catch, and Fig. 11 is the upright. In Fig. 12A you see this old-fashioned trap, set and ready for business. A small door in the box will make it easy to remove captives.

You may capture these little fellows by hand, if you use due caution in approaching their habit_ion, and shield your hand with an ordinary pocket-handkerchief.

They will make beautiful pets, and you will find them much more interesting than the common white mice.

Give them a tall narrow cage, with plenty of head room, wire a branch containing a last summer's bird's-nest to the side of their cage for sleeping quarters, and feed the mice with bread, seed, and grain.

Short-tailed Meadow-Rats

frequent the salt meadows, where their grass-roofed paths may be found intersecting each other everywhere. After the blunt-headed little creatures have been discovered, by uncovering their runways, you may capture them with your hand, shielded by a cloth cap.

Beware of their teeth, for they are savage biters and plucky fighters.

Meadow-rats are not climbers. Put them in a flat cage with a good wide expanse of bottom covered with sod of growing grass, the roots of which they will eagerly devour. Feed them garden vegetables, when grass roots are not available.

If you are an expert it is sometimes possible to catch chipmonks by hand. I never succeeded but once in capturing one in this manner. They will enter almost any ordinary sort of a trap, and can be best captured in that way. Set the trap near the hole known to be occupied by one of these scolding little rodents, and give your captives a roomy cage, with a dark corner for a nest. They make gentle and amusing pets. Feed them on acorns and nuts. Crack the hardest nuts for them.

Jumping-mice,

when discovered, are off like a flash, and are too swift of foot to be captured by hand—at least this has been my experience. They may sometimes be found under clods of an old ploughed field, in fence corners, or under loose brush and stones. Like the white-footed mice and flying-squirrels, they are nocturnal in their habits, and there may be thousands living all around you, and you will never suspect their presence until your cat brings one in from the field, or you find their half-devoured remains in the screech-owl's nest in the old apple-tree.

Jumping-mice have been known to make their nests in a beehive, and I know of one short-tailed meadow-rat which chose the same sort of sweet home.

In winter the jumping-mouse becomes torpid and apparently dead, and you may lay him away in a box of cotton, where it will remain until the bursting bud and freshening grass announce the approach of spring. Then your little pet will wake up, and be as full of life as if it had only taken a noon nap.

Although quite vicious, and dangerous to handle in their wild state,

Woodchucks

make very gentle and comical pets. One celebrated woodchuck-hunter had great success by using a stuffed woodchuck as a decoy. A very good substitute for a stuffed animal may be made of gray Canton flannel, stuffed with cotton.

Set your decoy up in plain view of the woodchuck's hole, and sprinkle fresh clover around. Then conceal yourself behind the hole, and be ready with a strong ring-net on a pole to capture your game when it appears.

The watchful old fellow will see the decoy sitting on its haunches, and reasoning that where it is safe for one "chuck" it is safe for another, he will sally forth to enjoy the clover. Then the fun begins. You must jump between

FIG. 13.   FIG. 13½.

FIG. 13.—The Wooden Box-Trap.—Dotted lines show arrangement inside. **A** is the trigger, or spindle, which passes through a hole in the rear end of the box. **B** is the catch with a ring slipped over its middle, to which a string is attached to hold open the trap-door when the trap is set. There is a notch in the back board of the trap at C, and another near the rear end of the trigger, in which the bevelled edges of the catch are caught and held in place by the string attached to the trap-door. Fig. 13½ shows the details of Fig. 13. The box-trap is an old "stand-by" with the boys, is simple in construction, and can be made by any lad who can handle tools. This drawing was made from a trap built by a country lad, twelve years of age. A serviceable trap can be improvised from an old tin can, or, better still, one of those square tin boxes used so generally now for holding fancy groceries.

the woodchuck and his hole, and net him as best you can, after which transfer him to a meal-bag, and carry him to his cage.

Woodchucks can run rapidly for eight or ten yards, then they have a habit of suddenly coming to a stop, assuming their favorite upright pose, and darting off again in another direction.

June is the time to capture the young ones, as they play about their home hole.

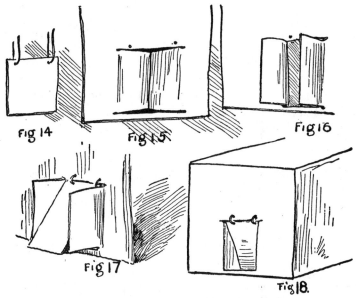

The Tin Can-Trap.—Make a door of a square or rectangular piece of tin. With a nail make two holes in the top of the door for the wire hinges (Fig. 14). With a heavy knife cut a doorway a trifle smaller than the door. Cut three slashes as shown in Fig. 15. Bend the two sides in as shown in Fig. 16, then hang the door with the wire hinges. Fig. 17 shows the door from the inside of the tin box, and Fig. 18 shows the same from the outside. The door, as may be readily seen, can be pushed up from the outside to admit the game, but when the prisoners attempt to get out they cannot push the door open, for the trap opens but one way. Do not leave space enough below the side-pieces for the animal to thrust his nose or paws under, or it may lift the door in this way and escape. If, as in the diagrams, it is necessary to cut a little above the bottom of the box, put a flat stone, or some similar object, inside for the side-pieces and the door to rest upon. Fig. 19 shows the manner of cutting the tin. Another door can be made by cutting a star in the tin, and then bending the pointed pieces in far enough to allow the game to squeeze through. The points will not allow anything to crawl out, however, and it must remain there until released (Fig. 20). These diagrams are given so that the young hunters may make their own traps, in case the ordinary mice and rat-traps to be found in shops are inaccessible.

A Box-Trap, or Figure Four,

may be successfully used to capture both young and old.

However fierce an old wild "ground-hog" may be, one that is taken young and reared in captivity is remarkably gentle. It is fond of a noonday nap, but when the sun sinks in the west, and the long shadows creep across the fields, it will rouse from its slumber, sit up, wash its face like a mouse or a squirrel, and be ready for a frolic.

When cold weather approaches, the woodchuck, ground-hog, marmot, or *siffleur*, as it is variously called, will prepare for a long winter sleep by rolling itself into a ball. In

FIG. 19.—How the Tin is Cut.

this condition you may pack it away like the jumping-mouse, and when friends call you can take the ground-hog out and even roll it around the floor without seeing any signs of life displayed by the hairy ball. But when spring returns, your Rip Van Winkle pet will awaken, and after sitting up on its haunches, and washing its face with its front paws, will be ready for a breakfast of clover or other food.

Rare old Captain John Smith, in his quaint "History of New England and the Summer Isles," published in London in 1624, gives, probably, the first written account of the musk-rat. He says that "the mussascus is a beast of the form and nature of our (English) water-rat;" and he adds, "some of them smell exceedingly strong of musk." These animals may be caught in almost any sort of a trap baited with sweet apples or parsnips.

Musk-Rats

have very strong teeth, and can use them on wood effectively, so it is wise to protect all corners and cracks in your wooden traps with pieces of tin or sheet-iron. They have good noses, and can smell an apple a long distance off. Place your traps in the shallow water at the edge of the mill-pond or stream inhabited by these rats, and they will doubtless find it without difficulty.

Young musk-rats are very gentle and playful, and may be handled without fear; they do not grow fierce with age if reared in captivity and accustomed to gentle treatment.

When kept in confinement give them a roomy cage, with a tank of water to swim in. Build the tank after the manner of the one described in the "Back-yard Fish-Pond."

FIG. 20.—The Tin Box-Trap.

There is one other little animal, familiar to most boys, and which they are too apt to value only for its skin. In truth, this creature generally has a very bad name, and, personally, I owe it a grudge for stealing all my live bait, on more than one occasion.

Nevertheless, when domesticated and supplied with plenty of food, like many a poor two-legged wretch, it will turn honest, and give up its bad habit of robbing hen-roosts. This long-bodied little animal is the mink, which, like those animals already described, is not difficult to capture in almost any sort of a trap.

When caught young it becomes very gentle, and even affectionate. It is passionately fond of frogs, and these batrachians make a good bait for mink-traps. Minks will eat fish, and when domesticated will not hurt your chickens, but will wage a relentless war upon rats and mice.

You need not confine your mink, for it will make chums of your dog and cat, and is fond of a cosey spot in the chimney corner.

While I was sketching on the coast of Maine I spent a whole day at my easel, between two great rocks. I soon

FIG. 21—Turtle-Trap.—This is simply a box with a door, like Fig. 10. The trap is set in shallow water, and baited with meat. It is very effective.

discovered that I was watched by some creatures, and it was not long before my neighbors made up their minds that the two-legged thing was a harmless sort of animal, and, before I finished my sketch, they amused themselves by jumping back and forth over my feet. At first I was more afraid of them than they were of me, but soon discovered that they meant no harm : so I painted away, with a pair of wild mink playing about my feet like tame kittens.

CHAPTER III.

THE BACK-YARD ZOO.

THE king of beasts and the royal Bengal tiger are neithei of them able to inspire such universal terror among the wiiq creatures of the forest as does man.

Bitter experience and terrible examples of man's ferocious cruelty to all wild animals have taught even the most humble and inoffensive of them to dread the approach of the bloodthirsty two-legged destroyer.

It is high time that we redeem

Our Reputation among the Brutes.

It is time we ceased our wasteful, senseless slaughter of every wild thing to be met with in field and forest. It is time we began to study live animals, in place of uncanny dried skins and badly upholstered "specimens," so-called.

This Gory Method of Study

belongs to the past. A new era has commenced, and real naturalists now drop their dry bones and moth-eaten skins to enjoy the study of live, healthy animals.

The boy who is really fond of animals never ill-treats his pets, or abuses and makes a slave of his dog. On the contrary, his dog is his companion and playmate.

The boy knows that a dog's master is a god in the eyes of the poor brute, and is

33

Worshipped with Canine Devotion,

which again and again has been proved faithful unto death. Such knowledge makes the boy just and kind. But a dog is only a domesticated wolf, and the wolf is not the only wild creature which can be domesticated; neither is the wolf the only animal which

Can Appreciate Kindness.

The same care which transforms a red-mouthed wolf into a faithful dog can transform other undomesticated beasts into useful creatures. As soon as an animal learns that you are contributing to its comfort, you may notice it will greet you with a milder expression. As soon as you can make the wildest and fiercest beast understand that the use of jaws, claws, or sting is unnecessary, it will refrain from using them. It is not always possible to come to this understanding with the larger beasts, and such animals are not fitted for back-yard zoos.

A lad who loves his pets will bestow upon the little creatures that affection which shows itself in a sympathy which can understand their wants and necessities. Such a lad can perform wonders; birds will come at his call, the small beasts of the field will follow at his heels, and no child will fear him.

Unfortunately, in spite of the amount of land on this continent, it is difficult for any but the very wealthy to have access to much of it, hence many readers will say, " We have no yard in which to keep pets," or, " Our yard is too small." Of course, if you are living in a flat you must go without a zoo, but if you have a yard it will probably not be less than twenty-five feet wide, and Fig. 22 shows how a very com-

Visiting the Animals.

prehensive zoo can be placed in the rear of a twenty-five foot lot, without materially interfering with such domestic matters as the drying of clothes on wash-day. A city

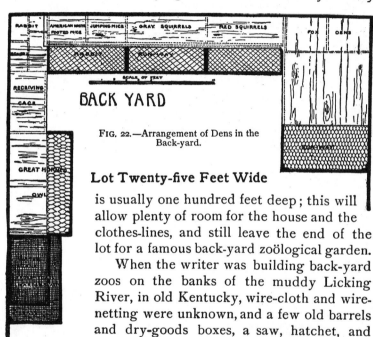

FIG. 22.—Arrangement of Dens in the Back-yard.

Lot Twenty-five Feet Wide

is usually one hundred feet deep; this will allow plenty of room for the house and the clothes-lines, and still leave the end of the lot for a famous back-yard zoölogical garden.

When the writer was building back-yard zoos on the banks of the muddy Licking River, in old Kentucky, wire-cloth and wire-netting were unknown, and a few old barrels and dry-goods boxes, a saw, hatchet, and some nails, constituted the materials and tools with which he and his playmates made cages for pets, frog-ponds, and dove-cots.

The writer's

Crow and Dog did the Bossing

of the work, and incidentally learned all the weak spots in the structures, a knowledge which they were not slow to use when the sheds and coops were finished, and occupied by creatures fascinatingly interesting to crows and dogs.

But you boys are lucky fellows! Everything that youth wants is now on the market at reasonable prices. Wirecloth and galvanized wire-netting with double-twisted selvages, with meshes of any size to suit the occasion, and wire of any dimensions to suit the purpose, are now manu factured especially for the building of cages.

Galvanized Iron Wire-Cloth or Netting

comes in rolls, with either square or hexagonal mesh; in other words, the openings between the wires are in the form of a square, or are six-sided.

Wire is numbered from the very heavy, No. 000, which

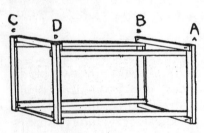

FIG. 23.—Temporary Frame of Cage.

is over a third of an inch in diameter, to No. 40, which is only .00725 of an inch in diameter. It is not very likely that you will use either of these wires, unless your collection includes some very large and strong beasts and some very small insects. The wires which you will probably need will be between No. 14 and No. 22. No. 14 is eighth-tenths of an inch in diameter, and No. 22 is a little more than two-tenths of an inch in diameter.

The Mesh

is the distance from *centre to centre* of the wire. No. 5 mesh means five meshes to the lineal inch—that is, a piece of netting five inches long will contain twenty-five meshes. The " space " means the opening between the wires—that is, the distance from *wire to wire.*

This is explained because some of the readers may not live near any dealer in wire-goods, and will be compelled to order what they want by letter. To do this intelligently they should understand the trade terms. Galvanized wire-netting, used for small bird-cages, comes in one-half, five-eighth and three-quarter-inch mesh, and is made of from No. 18 to No. 22 wire. The width of this netting varies from two feet to four feet. One-and-one-quarter-inch mesh is used for pigeon-houses, and the netting is from two feet to six feet wide. One-inch mesh is used for quail, ruffed grouse, pheasants, prairie-chickens, etc. A two-inch mesh is usually used for chicken-coops.

As a rule, the mesh which has square spaces is called wire-cloth, and that which has six-sided spaces is called netting. For mice, rats, chip monks, flying-squirrels, gray and red squirrels, use about No. $2\frac{1}{2}$ square mesh of No. 17 galvanized wire.

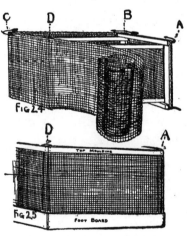

For woodchucks a nd musk-rats use a rather small mesh and pretty heavy wire, for their teeth are strong chisels, and you will be surprised to see what skilled mechanics they are in the use of the tools with which nature has supplied them. For rabbits, a two-inch mesh or any of the nettings used

FIGS. 24 and 25.

for poultry answers all purposes; but for foxes, if you use a two-inch mesh, be careful to have it of heavy wire. The writer's Skye terrier pup gnawed its way through the chicken-coop wire-netting on various occasions, and a fox has all the energy of a terrier, coupled with a most sur-prising amount of ingenuity and skill in jail-breaking.

A Pair of Foxes

I once owned could undo any knot or catch that I could invent with which to fasten them, and I was only made aware of the fact from the complaints of lost chickens which came from our neighbors.

While the neighbors were protesting, Faust and Mrs. Faust lay in front of their den, staring innocently at us with their great brown eyes, but investigation proved that the chains which apparently confined them were attached to nothing but their collars; and, furthermore, when I pushed the foxes aside with my foot, sundry quills and feathers, protruding from the fresh earth of their bed, showed only too plainly that our neighbors were not with-out reason in suspecting my innocent-looking rascally pets. I at last solved the problem by chaining the foxes together, and in spite of all their cunning, they never learned to go through the same opening in the fence, but each chose a different exit, and both were then held by their chain.

Each Cage

the reader makes will, of necessity, be of a form peculiar to his purpose and the location where it is placed. If it is for a fence-corner there will be but two sides to cover with wire-netting; if it be against the fence there will be three sides of netting: the fence forming the other side. In a hundred different ways will the surroundings modify the form of the cages, so, to simplify matters, we will suppose the proposed pen is to stand in the centre of the yard. In this case,

To Make a Cage of Galvanized Wire-Netting,

you first decide upon the wire and the mesh which are needed for this particular coop, next decide what are to be the dimensions; then, with a hand-saw, cut four wooden uprights exactly the same length, and fasten these posts together, temporarily, as shown in Fig. 23, A, B, C, D.

The strips connecting the uprights, and forming a box-like frame, should be only secure enough to keep the frame in shape. The nails in the strips must be driven just far enough to hold, leaving the head and enough of each nail above-board to render it a simple task to withdraw the nails when you wish to remove the strips.

FIG. 26.—Cages and Runway.

When the temporary frame or mould is finished (Fig. 23), fasten the end of the wire-netting securely to the front of the upright A with staple tacks, then pass the roll to B (Fig. 24), draw it tight, and with more staple tacks secure it to this upright; continue the same process at C and D, ending at A, as shown in Fig. 24. The arrows show the direction to be observed in passing the netting around the uprights.

When all is snug and fastened firmly, nail a footboard and top moulding on, as shown in Fig. 25, after which remove the temporary inside strips, and your coop is done. It has no roof or floor as yet, but the roof can be made of

wood or netting, as the occasion may require; the floor
may be of wood or earth, to suit the purposes for which it
is to be used.   In large cages the doors must be framed
and set in, as shown in the picture of fox-dens in the illustration of the back-yard zoo, but in small cages a small hole
may be cut in the netting—this can be done with an old
pair of shears.   The square piece of netting from the cut
can then be used as a door by fastening one edge with loops
of wire to the edge of the opening just made.   Picture-wire
and copper wire are best for such purpose, because they
are pliable and easily handled.

The Door

can, if desired, be made very neat by the following method:
Cut some tin into strips of the proper dimensions, then fold
the strips on their centre, lengthwise.   Punch a series of
holes by placing the folded strips of tin on a block of wood
and driving a nail through.   Slip the folded tin over the
exposed edges of the wire-netting, and sew it in place by
threading a fine wire through the holes.   Bind the edges of
the door in the same manner, then put a loop of wire on the
door for a hasp, and a smaller one on the cage near the edge
of the doorway for a staple, and the door may be fastened
with a peg of wood or a nail; or, better still, wire a hook on
the door in place of a hasp, and arrange it so as to hook
into the loop on the cage.

   It is often handy to have doors in the roof of a cage, as
in the roofs of the gnawers' cages, over the rabbit runway,
in the illustration.

The Doors for the Runway

to the rabbit-house are on top, and open like a door to a
bin, as shown in the illustration and in Fig 26.   While we

are at the rodents', or gnawers', quarters, it is well to remember certain peculiarities about the habits of these animals. Rats, mice, squirrels, and their kind, will invariably
seek a crack, angle or corner to commence work for a hole;
knowing this, it is well to protect all such places by pieces
of metal or tin, and none of the little fellows will make his
escape, unless the door is left open.

Rabbits will seldom gnaw out, but if they have an opportunity they will tunnel out.

To prevent diggers from escaping, allow your wire-netting to extend a foot and a half underground, below the footboard.

A Reptile House

need not be more than three feet high. It is not shown in
the illustration, but may be built as described and shown in
Figs. 23, 24, and 25, after which a roof of wire-cloth must be
added.

Into this house you put your turtles, frogs, toads, lizards, and snakes, and as most, if not all, of these require
water in considerable quantity, it is well to have a tank for
their use. But as every boy does not know how to build
the tank, he may learn by following the directions in the
following chapter, describing a back-yard fish-pond.

Be careful to set the tank level and pack it around with
good hard earth. It is well to sod the ground on three
sides, and cover the earth on the remaining side with clean
sand and gravel.

There should be a strip of land at least two feet wide
all around the tank, as a runway. When this is all arranged spread a layer of sand all over the bottom of the
tank, fill it with water, and place the cage over all. You
should have

An Old Piece of Canvas,

or some similar covering, for the cage, to be used when
your sand is in danger of being washed away by a down-
pour of rain.

Everything is now ready, and you can turn loose in the
enclosure

Your Whole Collection

of frogs, toads, lizards, and snakes, and they will soon
make themselves at home. You must not be surprised if
your pets in this cage feed upon one another. I once
owned an old bull-frog who would attempt to swallow anything that moved, with the exception of snakes. This frog
swallowed two live mice in one day, but he did not get
hungry again for two weeks.*

There are but few poisonous snakes in our country, and
in the Northern States we have but two kinds—copperheads
and rattlesnakes. Neither of these will add to the interest
of your collection, and must be left out and let alone.†

There are many beautiful and harmless little snakes to
be found in every field. They abound within the city limits of New York.‡ I saw two sunning themselves on a
neighbor's lawn, and discovered their home in the gate-
post.

You will be surprised at the many varieties of frogs you
can find when you start to collect these comical little creat-

---

* An account of this frog is in "The American Boy's Handy Book."

† The South has also the venomous water-moccasin or cotton-mouth, and the
poisonous but timid coral and harlequin-snakes.

‡ Snakes in neighborhood of New York: Dangerous—Banded rattlesnake, cop-
perhead. Harmless, can be domesticated—Black-snake, worm-snake, ringnecked-
snake, black pilot-snake, green-snake, water-snake, brown-snake, hognosed-snake
(adder), milk-snake, garter-snake, ribbon-snake.

ures. Some of them are very difficult to catch, and they often turn up in the oddest of places. I found a big toad in the top of a tree which I had climbed after young crows. It was a common hop-toad, not a tree-frog.

Silly Superstitions of Hoop-Snake Age.

It is high time that the American boys, in the dawn of the twentieth century, should forget all the fabulous stories of snakes with the power to "charm" persons, toads with death-dealing breath, deadly swifts and venomous lizards. All such yarns are handed down to us by our superstitious

Chipmonk. White-footed Mouse. Short-tail Meadow-Rat.

ancestors, and are a part of the witch belief of the old Salem folk. There are people living now who will tell you that they have seen a hoop-snake with his tail in his mouth, rolling down hill, and these people really believe what they say; but so did the Salem folks believe in witches.

Toads : Useful and Harmless.

If our comical, insect-destroying toads were venomous, the hand which pens these lines would have perished while it was still a chubby, dimpled, baby's hand.

Neither Do Toads Make Warts;

otherwise the writer's hands would be far too warty to wield either a pen or a brush; but in spite of the hundreds of toads handled by the writer he never was afflicted with warts on either hands or body.

In Pennsylvania there is a toad which has occupied the same back-dooryard for over ten years, and he will eat his own weight in " bugs " in a very short time.

The funniest toad ever owned by the writer was a Kentucky hop-toad with five well-developed legs, and the largest frog the writer ever caught was a New York bull-frog, which weighed one pound.

Frog Market.

St. Paul and Minneapolis are the great frog markets of the world. The receipts there last year, according to the daily papers, were something over six million frogs!

In the neighborhood of New York City one of the earliest frogs is the little brown cricket-frog. Next come the mysterious and shrill-voiced peepers, which make each marshy spot fairly shriek with their high-keyed notes.

Peepers

are hard to capture, because you can seldom see them. A dip-net run through the water where you have heard peepers will generally reward you with two or three little dusky imps, who, when captured, will sing in your coat-pocket, and the writer has had them sing while imprisoned in his hands.

A loud, coarse trill announces the appearance of

The Tree-Toad,

and this batrachian makes a most interesting addition to the collection. It is said that the tree-toad has the power of changing color, varying from ash-white, dull-gray or a brown to a bright-green hue.

You must look for the hermit-frogs or spade-frogs where they hide in holes in the ground, and in the damp wood you can hunt the lean-flanked, beautifully-spotted leopard-frog, his cousin, the pickerel-frog, and the brown wood-frog.

The bright-green-tree specimen, known as

The Anderson Frog,

is considered by frog-hunters as a great prize, and specimens can only be captured at rare intervals. When you secure a rare frog do not put him in the same place with larger frogs, for the latter will swallow their smaller companions the first time they feel hungry.

The Frog Has Teeth.

Put your finger in a frog's mouth and you can distinctly feel a number of fine, sharp teeth, but if you put your finger in a toad's mouth you will find no teeth; a frog grabs his prey with his jaws, a toad snips it up with his tongue.

Besides the common, funny old hop-toad, there are the Rocky Mountain hop-toads, the Southern hop-toads, and the hop-toads from Northeastern Massachusetts, which differ sufficiently from the common hop-toad to be classed by naturalists as sub-species.

Lizards.

With the exception of the Gila Monster *there are no poisonous lizards known,* and although many of the little creatures will try to bite you, their teeth are as harmless as so many needle points, and cannot be felt through a glove. Put on an old glove when handling them and you can hold them better; but be very careful and not be rude, or you may be surprised to find you have a stump-tailed lizard in your hand while the caudal appendage will be twisting around in a most astonishing manner at your feet.

Many beautiful and interesting lizards may be captured in all parts of the Union.

That it is not cruel to capture and confine wild animals is proved by the fact that almost all wild creatures, after they have become thoroughly familiar with their quarters, will not voluntarily leave their artificial homes for any protracted period. I have had wild pigeons return after giving them their freedom, and have had foxes return after securing their own freedom, by skill and cunning superior to that exercised by me in confining them. As for crows, coons, squirrels, and numerous other creatures possessed by me at different times, only death or forcible detention ever prevented them from returning to the place where plenty of food and kindness awaited them.

It is not necessary, or even desirable, to build all your cages at one time, for it is hardly possible that you will know just what you need until you have secured the creatures you wish to keep confined in the proposed pens and enclosures.

The Receiving-Cage.

Allow your cages to grow naturally, by adding additions or new ones as the occasion requires. Acting upon this plan the receiving-cage will be the first to be erected, and it should be strong enough to securely confine the largest of your captives, while the mesh of the wire-cloth should be fine enough to prevent the escape of the smallest pocket-mouse. The angles and corners should be well protected with metal, to resist the teeth of the gnawers, and the bottom protected with wire-cloth, to defeat the attempts of the diggers.

This cage will, at different times, furnish lodging for all the varieties of beasts or birds which are from time to time included in your ever-growing collection. Your new animals are first put in the receiving-cage, and must live there until suitable quarters are built for them.

The Value of Room.

Build all your cages as roomy as your available space and material will allow, and study to make their interiors as like the natural haunts of the imprisoned animals as is practicable. Avoid all attempts at ornamenting the cages, for no cage looks better and more artistic than the strictly practical one, built solely with a view to usefulness.

Clean sand will be found very useful for spreading over the floors of the wooden-bottomed cages, and a large box of it, kept in a dry place, will add greatly to your ability to keep things tidy.

Be particular about the nesting of your mice and squirrels; frequently remove the old nests and burn them, at the same time supplying the little creatures with a fresh lot of clean cotton, wool, fine grass, or even paper, and they will arrange a new bed for themselves out of the fresh material.

You will soon discover that all beasts prefer to keep clean, and have methods of their own by which they endeavor to keep themselves neat and presentable, without the use of soap. Any disagreeable odor proceeding from their cages simply means neglect on the part of the keeper of the zoo.

CHAPTER IV.

A BACK-YARD FISH-POND.

ALTHOUGH the writer has made frequent journeys to the wonderful dreamland of his boyhood, and has ruthlessly taken and brought to earth many of its air-castles for the use of the boys of the present day, there are still a number of things left, and among the latter is the back-yard fishpond, which we shall now seize, and, bringing the idea down to your back-yard, make it water-tight, so that you can stock it with real live fish.

A Shallow Pond,

with a broad surface exposed to the air will support, in health many more inhabitants than a deep hole, with small exposed surface. Remember that it is easier to keep a fish alive in a shallow basin than it is in a bottle holding exactly the same amount of water.

If You Dig a Hole

in your yard and fill it with water, it will be a mud-hole, in which no self-respecting fish will live: besides which the soil will soon soak up the water and leave the mud to bake in the hot summer sun.

By Sinking a Wooden Tank

in the ground and filling it with water a pond may be made. But any old box will not answer, for, unless you are a much

48

The Back-yard Fish Pond.

better mechanic than the writer was at your age, you will not be able to prevent an ordinary box from leaking.

However, if you really want a back-yard fish-pond, you may make a box or tank which will hold water, and the

Best Form for Such a Tank

is that of a wide, flat-bottomed scow. This scow may be of any dimensions you choose to build it, but I would advise

FIGS. 27 and 28.—The Side-boards must be Duplicates.

you to make your first one not more than six feet long by four feet wide, and two feet deep.

In selecting lumber for the scow, pick out pieces which are comparatively free from knots or blemishes. Reserve two one-and-a-half-inch planks, and keep the half-inch boards for the bottom.

A saw, a plane, and a sharp hatchet are necessary, but

other tools, if not absolutely needed, should not on that account be ignored, as they may come in very handy at times.

Trim off your two side-boards to exactly the same length—say six feet; they should then be six feet by two feet. On the edge which is to be the bottom measure toward the centre from each end of each board two feet, and mark the points; then rule a line diagonally from each of these points to the corners of the boards on the upper edge; this will mark out a sort of double-ended sled-runner, as shown in the illustrations, and when you saw off the triangular pieces marked on the boards you will have

Two Runners.

Set these runners side to side, on their long edges, and round off the angles with your plane, until the boards look like rockers (see Fig. 27). The side-boards must be exact duplicates of each other (Fig. 28).

Set the two side-pieces four feet apart and nail two or three temporary cross-pieces across their top (longest) edges to hold them in position; then turn them over and nail on the bottom-boards (Fig. 28).

You must use the greatest care in fitting the bottom-boards edge to edge, but you need not trouble yourself about the ends of the boards; allow them to project upon each side, as chance may direct. After the boards are all securely nailed to the bottom the ends may be sawed off flush with the sides of the scow (Fig. 29).

To Prevent the Wood from Decay

it is well to melt some tar over a fire, and, with a small mop made of rags tied to the end of a stick, paint the bottom of the scow with hot tar, being careful to see that all the cracks and crevices are thoroughly filled.

In the Shadiest Spot

you can find in the back-yard dig a hole for your tank. Make the bottom level. Set your tank in place and pack the earth well around the edges. Cover the bottom of the pond with about one inch depth of sand, and the surface of

FIG. 29.—The Ends may be Sawed off Flush.

the sand with a coating of gravel; then carefully fill the tank, without disturbing the sand, and allow the water to settle; after which a few aquatic plants may be introduced and a wire fence built around the pond to keep out intruders of the two-footed and four-footed kind. If you have a few small frogs and turtles the mesh of the wire in the fence must be small.

When to Stock.

After the water has stood for three or four days, and the aquatic plants have started to grow in their new quarters, you can stock the pond with sunfish, rock-bass, dace, small

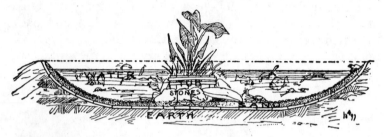

FIG. 30.—Cross-section of Tank.

catfish, crawfish, carp, and goldfish. The two last-named are the most stupid of the fish, and the rock-bass is one of the most intelligent fish I have ever kept in captivity.

Handy for the Pets.

The inclined ends of the scow-shaped tank give two sloping shores (Fig. 30), which will be appreciated by the crawfish, turtles, and frogs ; and if you build a little rockery in the centre the more timid fish will thank you for your thoughtfulness in providing them a safe retreat.

If it is possible for you to

Catch Your Own Fish

do not waste your money buying stupid goldfish. The fun of hunting for other small fish, capturing them and taming them, is more than half the pay for the work, in the pleasure it will afford you. However, if you are so situated that you cannot go fishing yourself, the aquarium stores in the big cities will supply you with almost any sort of aquatic creature.

Fresh-Water Clams

or mussels will live in confinement, and a few make an interesting addition to a collection. Water‑snails act as scavengers for the under-water settlement, and a handful of them may be added to form a sort of street-cleaning department. Caddice worms and the little fresh-water shrimp which you find among the water-plants make excellent food for your fish.

Avoid Salt-Water Sand,

stones, and shells, for the salts they contain are injurious to fresh-water creatures. Do not change the water in the tank after it is in running order; but as it evaporates replenish with fresh water.

CHAPTER V.

PIGEON-LOFTS AND BANTAM-COOPS.

THE best place in the world for boys is out-doors, breath-ing good fresh air, and the best place in the world for pigeons and chickens is out-doors, breathing good fresh air. Our modern environments too often limit the amount of out-door space which boys can occupy, and also limit the supply of fresh air they can furnish their pets.

In making designs for the latter we must take into con-sideration the limited space of a city back-yard, as well as the fact that during the extreme cold weather pigeons, chickens, and boys, all need some warm retreat where they may roost or sleep.

Indeed, chickens really

Need Shelter

more than either boys or pigeons; the former have been known to thrive and grow lusty and strong when living like the wild animals of the forests, and every boy knows of some location where pigeons have taken up their abode with no better shelter than that afforded by an open shed, or the overhanging eaves of a house.

Chickens,

coming originally from tropical woods, will thrive better where their delicate combs and toes are not liable to be frost-bitten, and one is more certain not to lose his fantails, pouters, ruff-necks, tumblers, and homing pigeons, if he has a suitable loft in which to confine his pets. These considerations lead to the designing of a combined pigeon-house and bantam-coop suitable for the limited space of the diminutive city back-yards, or even appropriate for the roof of a rear extension, where there is no back-yard to the dwelling.

FIG. 31.—Frame of Bantam-Coop and Pigeon-Loft.

By referring to Fig. 31 you will see two boys at work upon the frame of

A Pigeon-Loft and Bantam-Coop

which is capable of holding with comfort enough pets to gladden the heart of any healthy boy.

The longest posts, A G and B H, are supposed to be about nine or ten feet high and nailed fast to the back

fence. The dotted line, which cuts the frame in half, is to
show that a building half the size of the one in the drawing will be plenty large enough for quite commodious quarters for the birds. After the frame has been nailed together
and the protruding ends of the timbers all sawed off even
with the rest of the frame, a floor must be laid to the pigeon-
loft and securely nailed in place.

Rough Lumber Will Answer.

It is not even necessary to have smoothed lumber for
the flooring or any part of the house, but matched and
planed boards will make a much neater piece of work.
The uprights and all the frame are supposed to be built of
" two-by-four " (two inches thick by four inches wide), but
even this is not necessary, and in the country, where trimmed
lumber is scarce, the whole frame may be built of poles cut
in the woods.

When the

Pigeon-Loft Floor

is nailed down, set the door-jambs in place, between D J and
B H, and the window-jambs between D J and F L, as shown
by Fig. 32.   Nail the jambs fast to the rest of the frame, toe-
nailing the loft door-jamb to the floor of the loft, and the
coop jamb to the ceiling of the coop, also the two horizontal
jambs of the window-frame to the two upright jambs of the
same.

Shutter Frames.

Over the top-piece, C D, and the bottom piece, N, nail
two boards, each about six inches wide (R and S, Fig. 32),
and upon the inside of the loft erect three boards, one at
each end and one in the middle (facing the roof of the coop),
each of the same width as the top and bottom-boards. This

is to make a framework for the shutters, with which to close the loft in bad weather. Over the uprights just erected nail the strips, Q, O, and P (Fig. 32). Repeat this with the front end of the coop, E, F, K, and L, of Fig. 31, and you will have it as represented by Fig. 32.

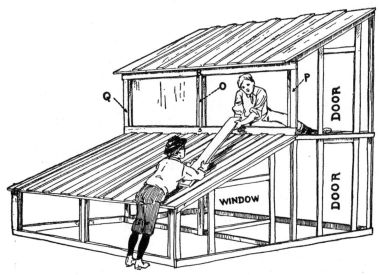

FIG. 32.—Framed and Roofed.

Roofing Material.

There are several cheap kinds of tar and gravel-paper sold which make neat and durable roofings, not only for coops and sheds, but even for more ambitious structures. In case these are not easily obtainable, roof the loft and coop with ordinary boards, using another lot of boards to cover the cracks between the first layer (Fig. 32).

It is now only necessary to nail on your sidings, and your loft-coop is finished, all but the doors and windows.

Dimensions are not given for these, because it often happens that there is some old window or hot-bed sash lying around the place, and the jambs can be made to fit the sash. The sash is held in place by nails, for it is not intended to open the window, the sash only being used to let light into the lower bantam-coop.

The open face of the pigeon-loft and bantam-coop are to

FIG. 34.

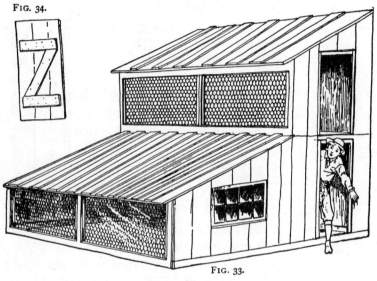

FIG. 33.

FIGS. 33 and 34.

be covered with wire-netting, fastened securely with staple tacks, inside the coop and loft, as shown by Fig. 33.

Doors.

Fig. 34 shows how to make the doors of boards, fitted together and secured by two cross-battens and one diagonal-batten.

When the doors are hung upon their hinges the house is finished, but not furnished. It is not necessary to have any protection for the screen fronts during the summer, but when winter comes four shutters, made to fit these openings, it will be found, will keep out the storms and protect the inmates from the cold.

The Shutters

may be made in the same manner as the doors, and hinged on to the lower sill of the loft, so that when open, during fair weather, they will rest securely upon the roof of the coop. The coop-shutters may be hinged in the same manner or simply fitted into place and held there by props of some sort, which, with the shutters, may be removed in fair weather, to admit the air and sunshine so dearly loved by your pets.

Keep Clean.

I take it for granted that you know how to care for the chickens and pigeons; that you know that no being, not even man, can keep himself clean and healthy when confined to a small room. The keeper must attend to all household duties.

If your pets are untidy, soiled in appearance, and their abode infested with parasites, it will be because of the cruel thoughtlessness of their keeper. To facilitate house-cleaning, Fig. 35 shows the internal arrangement and furniture of the coop-loft, all of which may be removed in a few moments and the whole place cleaned and whitewashed.

The Hen's-Nest

box is made with a steep slanting roof, which will prevent the chickens from roosting on the box. The latter has no bottom to it ; the nests rest upon the earth, so that you may pick up the box at any time, turn it upside down, and turn the hose on it, or plentifully plaster it with clean, wholesome whitewash.

Pigeon-Nests.

A cleat nailed to the inside wall of the loft, near the door, serves as a rest for one end of the pigeon-nests.   The other end is supported by a piece of wood about four inches wide which is hinged to the back wall, and its upper end held in place by a long hook made of a piece of telegraph wire.

If this hook is unfastened the wooden support falls down and the box of nests slips off the cleat into your arms.

Pigeons are not good at perching upon twigs or sticks. Their feet are adapted for walking upon flat surfaces, and they need a broad surface for a roost.   Fig. 40 shows how to make a pigeon-roost, which may be hung up against the wall by slipping the two holes bored in the top of the back board over a couple of nails in the wall.

For a Hen-Roost,

nail a narrow strip of wood, with its flat side upon the thin edge of another similar strip.   The end will then look like a T, Fig. 38.

Round off the edges of the perch with a plane or knife until it is of the form of the right-hand diagram.

Fig. 37 shows a roost of this kind. Fig. 36 shows the ad-justable side-rail, with slots for the perch to fit, and Fig. 39 shows a cleat to nail against the wall for the other end of the roost.   As may be seen, the perch will fit in the slot in the cleat.

Drinking-Troughs.

Figs. 41 and 42 are drinking-troughs, arranged so that the birds will not soil the water.

The jug-trough was made by a farm hand, friend of the writer. He made a hole near the bottom of the jug by first nicking off a piece of the hard glazed surface with the corner of a hatchet, and then drilling the hole with a sharpened nail. When the jug was filled with water, a stopper was put in and it was set in an old dish; the water remained above the hole in the jug, but rose no higher.

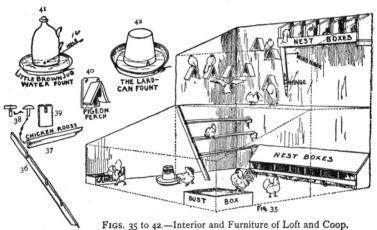

FIGS. 35 to 42.—Interior and Furniture of Loft and Coop.

Fig. 42 is an

Old Lard-Can,

with a triangle cut in the edge. Fill the can with water and place a dish over the top, hold the dish in place, and turn the can upside down, and the water will fill the dish and keep it filled to the top of the cut in the can as long as there is water in the can.

Flying-Cage.

By erecting posts at or near the lower end of the bantam-coop and stretching wire netting from post to post, and thence to pigeon-loft, a space can be enclosed and roofed over with netting, which will allow your pigeons room to exercise their wings. This arrangement does not neces-sarily use up a foot more ground space.

There are many other simple arrangements which these few will help to suggest to the reader, and which will add to the comfort and happiness of his pets.

CHAPTER VI.

HOW TO MAKE A BACK-YARD AVIARY.

IT was before the directors of the Brooklyn Institute had met with success in their silly work of introducing the house-sparrow (known here as the English sparrow) to this country, and long before these foreign pests were spread over the length and breadth of the United States, that the court-house in Covington, Ky., was surmounted by a wooden image of George Washington.

Bird's-Nests in Washington's Coat.

All boys know that Washington loved his country, but few know that he was a bird-fancier. That the father of our country loved the native birds is attested by the fact that they built nests in the wooden wrinkles of his sleeves and in the hollow ends of the roll of parchment which he held in his hand. His favorite bird was the red-headed woodpecker. He had it on the brain, and although each year a brood of little red-headed birds were hatched in his head, the dear old patriot never made a wry face, but with a benign smile he gazed over the roof of the livery stable across the street.

Bird's-Nests in Speaking-Horn.

Upon the same lot with the court-house stood the fire-engine-house, with its old-fashioned lookout tower. On the top of the tower was a weather-vane, made of a great fire-

63

man's horn, but the only voices which ever issued from this old speaking-trumpet were the voices of the purple martins, singing their bubbling love songs, the twittering of their mates, or the impatient piping of the young birds inside their revolving home.

It was in the swinging, moving weather-vane of the engine-house that these birds each year built their nests and reared their young.

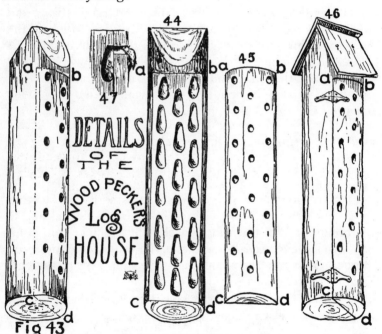

FIGS. 43 to 47.—The Log may be Rounded or Square.

A Woodpecker's House.

There is an army of interesting birds called creepers, sapsuckers, and woodpeckers, which no one has, apparently, thought of providing with homes, yet it is not difficult to suit the woodpeckers with houses.

A substitute for their favorite rotten tree or stump may be made of a sound piece of timber. The log may be squared or rounded, as in nature (Fig. 43). Saw off the bottom so that the log may set upright, then trim off the top end wedge-shaped, to shed the rain or to receive a roof, which will still further protect it from the weather.

Next saw a deep cut as shown by the dotted line, A, B. With a large-sized auger bore a number of holes in the face of the log; these holes must be bored deep enough to leave a slight indentation in the main part of the log after the piece, **a, b, c, d,** has been removed.

After the holes are bored begin at **c, d** and saw to **a, b** (Fig. 43), and lift off the piece **a, b, c, d** (Fig. 45).

With chisel and gouge cut out the nest holes. Make them about eight inches deep, as shown in Fig. 44. Fig. 47 gives a cross-section of the hole, showing it to be of the same form as those made by the birds themselves, in George Washington's head, or the old stump in the woods.

The Perforated Door

may now be replaced and spiked to the log, and the roof (Fig. 46) nailed on the top, which will complete the wood-pecker's home.

A better plan than spiking the door in place is to hang it on hinges, as shown in Fig. 46.

The Hinged Door

should be supplied with a padlock, as a safeguard against children and too-curious grown people. A handful of saw-dust thrown into the bottom of each nest-hole will supply

the place of the absorbent rotten wood to which these birds
are accustomed.

It is claimed that the English sparrow will not nest in a
swinging or moving house.   If this is true we may

FIGS. 48 and 49.—Bottle Gourds Hung
to Brackets.

Bring the Martins Back

by supplying them with
swinging houses made of
dipper and bottle gourds,
hung to brackets or to hoops
and poles (Figs. 48 and 49).

The Gourds for Bird's Houses

must be thoroughly dried,
and doorways cut in each,
near the bottom of the bowl.
Never make the entrance to
any sort of a bird-house on a
line with the bottom of the
house, for the nest will block
the doorway.

Paint the Gourds

bright red, green, blue, and yellow, and fasten the small
ends to the supports with copper wire, as shown in Figs. 48
and 49.

The Wren-House

shown in Fig. 50 is made of a grape-basket, and will not
stand rough weather, but if put in a sheltered place it will
last a long time.   Wrens love to build under a roof of any
sort.

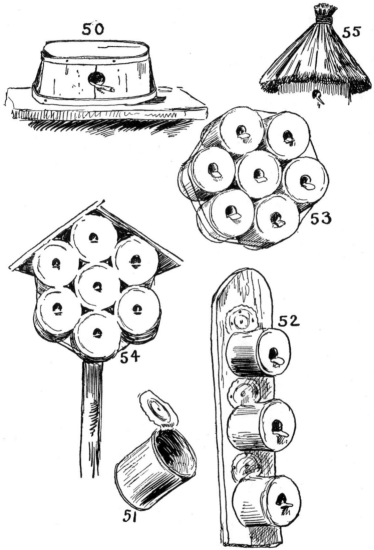

FIGS. 50–55.—Made from Fruit-Cans.

Tin-Can Bird-Houses.

Fig. 51 is an old fruit-can. Fig. 52 is the same nailed to a board. These tin cans may not appear beautiful when nailed to tree or shed, but if neatly painted and wired together (Fig. 53) they will present a most attractive appearance. Fig. 54 is a nest of cans, roofed. If a bunch of straw is bound firmly together, and the opposite ends spread over the bird-house (Fig. 55), it will make a very attractive thatched roof.

A House of Straw.

A pretty and durable house may be made by binding straw around hoops, and roofing the structure thus made with a bunch of straw.

Figs. 56, 57, and 58 explain the structure of

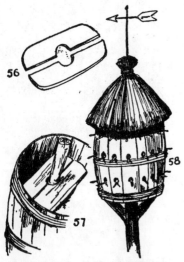

FIGS. 56-58.—A Thatched Barrel.

A Barrel for a Martin-House

which, when neatly made and thatched with straw, is decidedly ornamental, and will be duly appreciated by your bird friends.

If we can keep the English sparrows away, the bluebirds will nest in any sort of a sheltered hole.

Earthenware flower-pots, as shown in Fig. 59, may be used for bird-houses if you enlarge the holes in their bottoms to serve as doorways, and enclose the upper

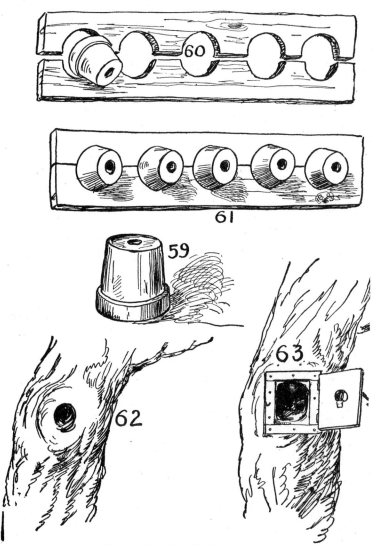

FIGS. 59–63.—From Earthenware Pots.

part between two boards (Figs. 60 and 61) which have previously had places cut out to receive the pots. If any of
your shade or fruit-trees have

Old Knot-holes

in them (Fig. 62), the rotten wood can be cleaned out, a
frame nailed around the opening, and a neat little door (Fig.
63) put on the frame.

The door should have a hole through it, with a perch or
stick attached, and this will make an ideal bird-house.

An Available Supply of Moist Clay

will often induce the cliff-swallows to plant a colony in your
neighborhood, and holes made in the gable ends of your
stable will invite the social barn-swallow to build under the
protecting roof.

Do not fail to keep fresh water, in shallow pans or earthenware dishes, on your lawn, for bird baths.

At my suggestion Samuel Jackson, my young brother-
in-law, set out baths upon the lawn last summer, and the
photograph on the opposite page is one which he took of
a wild robin enjoying his free bath.

There is another

Little Native American

friend which the noisy sparrows are doing their best to
drive away.   This is the house-wren : as interesting and busy
a little mite as ever protected a garden from noxious insects.
If you make your wren-house door the size of a silver quarter
of a dollar no robber sparrow can enter to despoil the nest.

Of our seven common species of swallows, four are avail-
ing themselves of the opportunity offered by the barns for
nesting.

Wild Robin at His Bath.

Photographed from life by Samuel Jackson.

Barn-swallows build under roofs; cliff-swallows, under eaves ; the white-bellied-swallow and martin, in boxes set up for that purpose, when these shelters are not preëmpted by the English sparrows.

The native swallows destroy an amount of noxious insects beyond calculation, and almost beyond imagination. Without birds this world would, because of insects, be uninhabitable, yet each year two hundred millions of them are sacrificed *for women's hats and bonnets.* Aside from the inexcusable barbarity of this practice is its menace to our trees, our crops, and our very existence.

CHAPTER VII.

A BOY'S BACK-YARD WORKSHOP.

How to make Buildings Plumb and Level.

By a workshop is meant a place where a boy can build a boat, sled, box-kite, man-kite,* mend a golf-club, a broken bicycle, his mother's rocking-chair, his aunt's umbrella, or build a paper-balloon.† It is a room, house, or shed, where a boy can do what pleases him, without being in everybody's way ; a place where he can retire and idly whittle a stick, or seriously work out some youthful invention ; a place where he can entertain his young friends during the rainy or stormy days of winter, and where they can talk over the new football team, baseball or golf club, without being oppressed with the knowledge that their loud talk is annoying the older folks.

The late war has demonstrated to the whole world the wonderful skill and pluck of the young American, and the world must not suppose these qualities to be suddenly acquired, but must know them to be a matter of education —an education acquired during boyhood, at the boy's own school, with boy professors.

The Success of Americans

is not on account of any peculiarity of the blood which flows in their veins, but because they live under a govern-

---

* For description and diagrams see "The Outdoor Handy Book."
† "The American Boy's Handy Book."

ment which teaches independence, and the boys on the play-ground become self-reliant, resourceful lads, developing their skill by building kites, sleds, and boats, and developing their pluck on the baseball and football field.

To such youths it is unnecessary to enumerate the advantages of a workshop; neither is it essential to point out to them the fact that they may commence their collection of tools with a serviceable pocket-knife.

A Good Oil-stone,

to keep the knife sharp, is a prize, and for its protection from dust or injury it should be set into a block of wood so that about one-eighth of an inch of the stone projects above the block. A similar block, with a space the size of the stone and one-eighth of an inch deep cut out of its centre, should be made for a cover.

A Hatchet

is not a difficult thing to procure, and a saw, a screw-driver, a gimlet, and a three-cornered file can be added to the collection as opportunity offers. Next a chisel or two, and you will have a kit of tools with which, if skilfully used, you can build anything from a three-legged stool to a flying-machine.

Use the Best Tools You Can Get.

With an axe or hatchet, an auger and a sheath-knife, the whole race of pioneers, including Daniel Boone, Davy Crockett, and the parents of Abraham Lincoln, built their homes and made their household furniture.

It is not to be supposed that any boy, in his right mind, will prefer an old dull auger, blunt axe, and a butcher-knife to a chest of bright, new, modern tools, but unless a boy belongs to the Miss Nancy, Little Lord Fauntleroy type, he will do his best with the implements at hand, and acquire better ones as the occasion offers. In this manner the contents of his tool-chest will grow gradually, and keep pace with the development of his skill as a mechanic.

Such a lad, when in need of

A Level,

will make himself one, probably using three pieces of board, a string, and a weight, as shown in Fig. 64. The

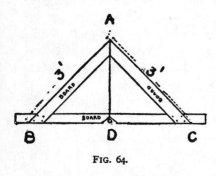

FIG. 64.

two side-pieces of wood being exact duplicates in all dimensions, the angles at the bottom are necessarily equal, and a line from the apex (A) to the centre of the bottom-piece must be a plumb line. After sawing out his side-boards and joining them at their top edges, he nails a straight piece to the bottom-ends, using the utmost care to have the lower edge of the bottom-board exactly the same distance from A on each arm; that is, A B must be exactly the length of A C, and B D must equal D C. He next cuts a small notch at A, so that he can fit a string at the crack between the two arms, A B and A C. A notch is also cut at D, to allow the weight play-room. When the lower edge of the bottom-board is placed upon a level, and the string ceases to vibrate, it will be found that, the bullet hanging free, the string exactly covers a line which has been previously ruled across the bottom-board. The line was ruled by placing a straight-edge, or rule, at A and D. The slightest incline of the base-board will throw the string to one side or the other, and show the base to be out of level.

This implement is a simple thing to construct, is as serviceable as a spirit-level, and as reliable.

For buildings, a large-sized level, with side-pieces three feet long, is useful. Smaller ones are handy in the shop.

A Convenient, Home-Manufactured Plumb

is made by dividing a straight piece of board with a black line, exactly in the centre, extending from end to end. This piece is notched at one end in the same manner as the previous one, and a string and weight attached, as shown by Fig. 65. By placing the edge of this against a wall it can be determined whether it is in or out of plumb.

The boy who can manufacture these two tools can, with the aid of other boys, build himself

FIG. 65.

A Workshop;

and it is possible he can do it alone, but when it comes to lifting heavy lumber he will be glad of the assistance of some of his friends.

If the reader is the happy possessor of some old locust fence-posts, he has the best sort of material for a foundation Lacking locust, chestnut posts will make a good substitute. Lacking chestnut, some carefully laid and levelled stones or bricks will answer all purposes. I have seen many an old house resting upon four heaps of rough stones, the latter having faithfully supported the edifice for years, and prevented the sills from rotting from contact with the damp earth.

Even the ground will answer for

A Foundation,

if the dirt is properly packed and drained. All through
certain sections of this country there are hundreds of humble dwellings built upon " mud-sills "—in other words, with
no other foundation or floor but the bare ground.

I will, however, suppose that you have secured some
posts about two feet six inches long and with good flat ends.

The better the material you can obtain, the trimmer and
better will be the appearance of your house ; but a house

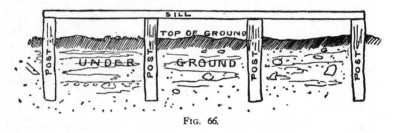

FIG. 66.

which will protect you and your tools may be made of the
roughest of lumber.

The plans drawn here will answer for common or fine
material, but we will suppose that medium material is to
be used. It will be taken for granted that the reader is
able to procure enough two-by-four-inch timber to supply
studs, ribs, purlins, rafters, beams, and posts, for the frame
shown in Fig. 69. Two pieces of four-by-four-inch timber,
each fifteen feet long, should be procured for sills. If this
is inaccessible, two pieces of two-by-four nailed together
will make a four-by-four sill. Add to this some tongue-and-
grooved boarding for sides and roof, some enthusiasm and
good American pluck, and the shop is almost as good as built.

How to Build the House.

First lay out the foundation, eight feet by fifteen; see that the corners are square—that is, at right angles; test this with a tape or string, by measuring diagonally from corner to corner both ways, and if it measures exactly the same you are all right, and may proceed to dig your post-holes. The outside of the posts should be flush, or even, with the outside edges of the sills and end-beams of the house, as shown in Fig. 66. There are to be four posts on each of the long sides of the house, at equal distances apart —a little less than five feet from centre to centre of each post.

Dig the holes two feet deep, allowing six inches of the posts to protrude above ground. If you drive two stakes a short distance beyond the foundation, in line with your foundation lines, and run a string from the top of one stake to the top of the other, you can, without much trouble, get

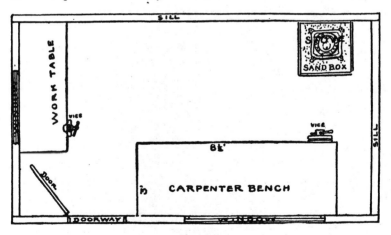

FIG. 67.

it upon a perfect level by testing it with your home-made level, and adjusting the stakes until the string represents the level for your sill.   When this is done,

Set Your Posts

to correspond to the level of the string, then place your sill on top of the posts, and test that with your level.   If found to be correct, fill in the dirt around the posts and pack it firmly, then spike your sill to the posts.   Go through the same operation with the oppo-site set of posts and sill.

FIG. 68.

The first difficult work is now done, and, with the exception of the roof, the rest only needs ordinary care, and what old-fashioned people used to term "gumption."

It is to be supposed that you have already sawed off and prepared nine two-by-four-inch beams, each of which is exactly eight feet long.   Set these on edge from sill to sill, equal distances apart, the edges of the end-beams being exactly even with the ends of the sills (Figs. 66 and 69).   See that the beams all cross the sills at right angles, and toe-nail* them in place.

You may now neatly

Floor the Foundation

with one-inch boards; these boards must be laid length-wise with the building and crosswise with the beams.

---

* Toe-nailing, or foot-nailing, consists in driving the nails diagonally or slant-ingly down through the ends of the beams to the sill, in place of nailing through from the top down to the sill.

When this is finished, you will have a beautiful platform on which to work, where you will be in no danger of losing your tools, and you may use the floor as a table, on which to measure and plan the sides and roof.

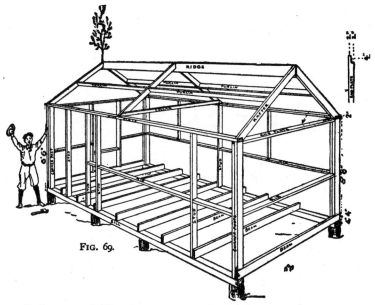

FIG. 69.

It is a good idea to

Make Your Ridge-Plank and Rafters

now, while the floor is clear of rubbish.

Lay out and mark on the floor, with a carpenter's soft pencil, a straight line, four feet long (A B, Fig. 70). At right angles to this draw another line, three feet six inches long (A D, Fig. 70). Connect these points (B D, Fig. 70), with a straight line, then complete the figure A B C D (Fig. 70). Now allow two inches at the top for the ridge-plank at B,

and two by four for the end of the side plate at D. You
then have a pattern for each rafter with a "plumb-edge" at
B and a "bird's-mouth" at D. The plumb-edge must be
parallel with B C, and the two jaws of the bird's-mouth
(Fig. 71) parallel with D C and A D, respectively. Make six
rafters of two-by-four-inch wood, one ridge-plank of two-
by-six or seven-inch wood.

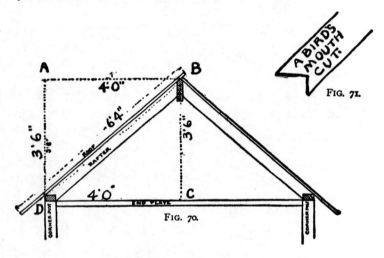

FIG. 71.

FIG. 70.

The "Purlins" and "Collar"

can be made and fitted after the roof is raised. Set your
roof-timber carefully to one side, and clear the floor for the
studs, ribs, and plates. First prepare the end-posts, and
make them of two-by-four. Each post is of two pieces (see
Fig. 69). There will be four outside pieces which rest on
the end-beams. These will be each five feet eight inches in
length, and four inside pieces, each six feet in length; this
allows two inches at the top for the ends of the end-plates
to rest upon.

Examine the Corner-Posts

in Fig. 69, and you will see that the outside two-by-four
rests partly upon the top of the end beam, and the side-
plate rests directly upon it. You will also observe that the
inside two-by-four rests directly upon the sill, which would
make the former four inches longer than the outside piece,
if it extended to the side-plate; but you will also notice
that there is a notch in the end-plate for the outside corner-
piece to fit in, and that the end of the end-plate fits on top the
inside piece of the corner-posts, taking off two inches, which
makes the inside piece just six feet long. This is a very
simple arrangement, as may be seen by examining the diagram. Besides the corner-posts, each of which, as we have
seen, is made of two pieces of two-by-four, there are four
studs for the front side, each six feet two inches long, and
one stud for the rear wall, six feet two inches long. The
short studs shown in the diagram (Fig. 69), on the rear side,
are unnecessary, and are only shown so that they may be
put in as convenient attachments for shelves and tool-racks.

The First Stud

on the front is placed two feet from the corner-post, and
the second one about six feet six inches from the first, to
allow a space for a six-foot window over the carpenter's
bench; the next two studs form the door-jambs, and must
be far enough from the corner to allow the door to open
and swing back out of the way. If you

Make Your Door

two and one-half feet wide—a good size—you may set your
last stud two feet from the corner-post, and leave a space

of two feet six inches for the doorway. Now mark off on
the floor the places where the studs will come, and cut out
the flooring at these points to allow the ends of the studs to
enter and rest on the sill. Next make four ribs—one long
one to go beneath

The Window,

one short one to fit between the corner-post and the door-
stud (not shown in diagram), another to fit between the
door-stud and the window-stud, and another to fit between
the window-stud and the first corner-post (the nearest corner in the diagram Fig. 69). Next make your

Side-Plate

exactly fifteen feet long. Fit the frame together on the
floor, and nail the pieces together, toe-nailing the ribs in
place. A lot of boys may now raise the whole side-frame,
and the ends of the studs can be slipped into their respective slots, the end-posts made plumb, and temporarily held
in place by a board, one end of which is nailed to the top
end of the post and the other to the end-beam. Such a
diagonal board at each end will hold the side in place until
the opposite side is raised and similarly supported.

It is now a simple thing to slip the end-plates in place
under the side-plates, until their outside edges are even
with the outside of the corner-posts and their notched ends
under the side-plates, and resting snugly upon the tops of
the inside pieces of the corner-post. A long wire-nail
driven through the top-plates and end-plates down into the
posts at each corner will hold them securely in place. Toe-
nail a rib between the two nearest end-posts, and make two
window-studs and three ribs for the opposite end. The
framing now needs only the roof-timbers to complete

The Skeleton of Your Shop.

Across, from side-plate to side-plate, lay some loose boards, for a platform; then, standing on these boards, let your assistant lift one end of the ridge-plank, while with one nail to each rafter you fasten the two end-rafters on to

FIG. 72.—Machine-Shop.

the ridge-plank, fit the jaws of the bird's-mouth cuts (Fig. 71) over the ends of the side-plates, and hold them temporarily in place with a "stay-lath"—that is, a piece of board temporarily nailed to rafter and end-plate. The other end of the ridge is now resting on the platform at the other end

of the house, and this may be lifted up, for the single nails
will allow movement and play to the posts.

The Rafters

are next nailed in place, with one nail each, and a stay-lath
fastened on, to hold them in place. Now test the ends with
your plumb-level, and when they are found to be correct,
nail all the rafters securely in place; stiffen the centre pair
with a piece called a collar (see Fig. 69).   Add four purlins
(Fig. 69), set at right angles to the rafters, and take off your
hats and give three cheers.

But do not forget to

Nail a Green Bough to your Roof-tree,

in accordance with the ancient and time-honored custom.
The sides of the house may be covered with the cheapest
sort of lumber, and roofed with the same material, but if
you can secure good stuff, use 13 × ⅞ × 9¼-inch tongue
and grooved, one side planed so that it may be painted ; you
can make two side-boards out of each piece six feet six
inches in length.   Nail the sides on, running the boards
vertically, leaving openings for windows and doors at the
proper places.

If you have made a triangular edge to your ridge-stick,
as in Fig. 70, it will add to the finish, and the roof may be
neatly and tightly laid, with the upper edge of one side
protruding a couple of inches over the opposite side and thus
protecting the joint from rain.   Additional security is gained
by nailing what are called picket-strips (⅞ × 1¾ inches)
over each place where the planks join.   Lack of space forbids me to go into many details, such as the manufacture of
the door and the arrangement of windows, but these small

problems you can easily solve by examining doors and windows of similar structures.

Figs. 67, 72, and 73 show the arrangement of the interior of the shop. Near the door and against the window is a work-bench with shelves, boxes, and tool-racks. This end of the room is called

The Machine-shop,

for here are the metal working-tools, wire springs, locks, bolts, nuts and all the odds and ends that are useful for mending anything, from a bicycle to an umbrella. Under the six-foot window is the carpenter's bench for carpenter-work.

FIG. 73.—Carpenter-Shop.

In Fig. 72 there is a

Tool-rack

across the front of the window for files, chisels, etc., but this is only a place to thrust the tools you happen to be

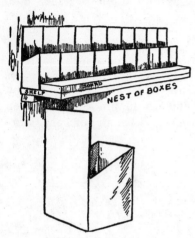

FIG. 74.—A Box.

using at the time. On account of the danger of rain from the open window, tools should not be left in the rack after the work is finished. In place of drawers, wooden boxes are made to fit loosely into compartments prepared for them. These boxes have wooden handles, as shown in the diagram, and they will be found very convenient. There is plenty of room under this work-table for more boxes when the accumulation of materials renders additional storing-room necessary. Sets of deep pigeon holes are very convenient for extra bicycle spokes and similar objects. Fig. 73 shows

The Carpenter's Bench,

and a few tools stored on the wall. A board with holes bored in it makes a good rack for hammers; saws should always hang in an accessible place, and ordinary brass or iron hooks may be used for this purpose.

To Protect your Auger-bits

from danger of rust, tack a piece of thick cloth or soft piece of leather to the wall, using sufficient material to allow a flap to hang down and cover the bits. Under the flap is a number of pockets, divided by stitching the front to the back-piece, or by tacking the division lines to the walls. (See the left-hand upper corner of Fig. 73.)

Care of Shavings.

A barrel or large box or basket should always be near the carpenter's bench to receive the shavings, and the stove must be set in a box of sand or earth, to prevent any danger of hot coals falling amid the easily ignited materials in the carpenter-shop. (Fig. 68.) The hole in the roof, where the stove-pipe goes through, must be protected by a sheet-iron ring or collar.

A Place for Tool-racks.

The blank wall, opposite the carpenter's bench, may be covered with tool-racks, shelves, and other arrangements for the convenience of the young workmen.

FIG. 75.   Rack Stick.

To Keep Small Things.

A number of old square tin boxes, such as certain firms use for packing cocoa, mustard, and various other food material, may be utilized by simply cutting off three sides, as shown in Fig. 74, and making a shelf with a depression for them to fit into, as shown in the sketch.

This makes a most convenient nest of boxes for screws, staples, and similar objects. Each box may be lifted out of

the rack by its long back and set where it is handy, until
you are through with it; then it may be replaced in exactly
the same spot, without trouble or annoyance.

Figs. 75 and 75a show

A Famous Old Rack,

which is familiar to all who have lived in the woods. It can
be made of the branch of any shrub or tree, with the aid of
a pocket-knife, and nailed to the wall as shown in Fig. 75a.

Moulding, boards, and picket-strips can be stored over-

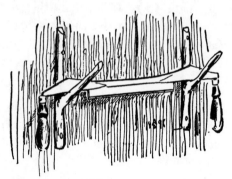

FIG. 75a.—The Famous Old Rack.

head, resting on the end-plates and the rafter-collar in the
middle of the roof.

This workshop has been planned so as not to crowd a
small back-yard, and if it is built of lumber which presents a
smooth outside it may be neatly painted, and will not injure
the appearance of the yard in the least. Vines may be
trained over the walls of the shop and flowers planted around
the outside, without in any manner interfering with its convenience as a workshop, or lowering the dignity of the
young artisans who make it their head-quarters.

CHAPTER VIII.

HOW TO BUILD AN UNDERGROUND CLUB-HOUSE.

THE muffled sound of voices, interrupted by peals of hollow laughter, issuing from the apparently solid earth, is a sufficiently startling phenomenon of itself; but when a group of boys and a dog suddenly emerge from the ground it is calculated to induce the most prosaic of persons to believe that the gnomes of fairy stories are, after all, living realities. For the peace of mind of all who may hear the mysterious voices and see the apparitions just described, it may be well to state that the gnomes are human and are members of the Bank-Swallows' Club, and if you hear their voices under your feet it is because you happen to be standing on the roof of their underground club-house.

These

American Gnomes

use only such magic as their healthy brains and sturdy arms can supply, and if they "cast a charm" upon you it will be one of the most delightful of all spells—the charm of boyhood!

The club-house may be built with

A Doorway at the Top

of the bank, concealed by a trap-door, or with an entrance from the hillside, as shown in the diagrams. If the reader chooses the first style he has simply to follow the diagrams here given, and reversing the proportions of the ventilator and entrance (Fig. 79), make an entrance of the vent and a vent of the entrance.

The Trap-Door

must be placed high enough above the surface of the ground to prevent the water from running into the house in wet weather, and a ladder should be provided, by which the boys may climb in and out of the house with ease.

Dimensions of the House.

The house should be big enough to allow room for a table and some chairs, stools, or benches, and the roof be so arranged that the tallest boy in the crowd may stand erect, with no fear of bumping his head.

The furniture must be placed inside the frame as soon as the floor is laid, because after the house is finished the entrance is too small to admit the passage of any object of more bulk than a creeping boy.

The hardest work is digging the foundation in the hill-side, but if six or seven boys take a hand at this, "for the fun of the thing," the work is soon done.

FIG. 76.—Cross-Section of Excavation.

Bank Swallows at Work.

A Cross-Section

is a picture showing how half an object looks. Fig. 76 is a cross-section of the excavation shown in Fig. 76a. The latter shows the finished foundation.

In Fig. 79 a cross-section of the earth-bank and

FIG. 76a.—The Excavation.

The Boys' Underground Club-House

is given, affording an idea of the proper proportions of the cave. When the foundation is entirely finished, collect your building material.

If you have

New Lumber,

use it ; if not, use old lumber, and if you are building in the woods the house may be built of logs and roofed with poles, covered with bark and boughs. The better the material the stronger will be the house. Secure some good sound planks and a supply of long strips two inches thick and four inches wide. Use two-by-fours for the frame of the house.

To give a

Pitch to the Roof,

to allow the water which filters through the dirt above to drain off at the eaves, make the rear posts, A, B and C, D (Fig. 77), exactly equal in length, but considerably longer than E, F and G, H, as in Fig. 79.

To add strength, erect another post midway between A, B and C, D.

Framing.

Cut the sticks A, C and B, D exactly equal in length and nail them to the uprights A, B and C, D, as in Fig. 77, using one nail at each corner; this will adjust the frame and make the four corners square, after which you may secure them in position by diagonal pieces similar to those shown on the end, A, E, B, F, Fig. 77. The corners may then be nailed. In nailing a temporary piece it is only necessary to drive the nails far enough to hold for the time.

Next make the frame E, G, H, F, and in the middle of this frame nail on the two door-jambs I, J, and K, L. While some of the boys hold the front and rear frames in an upright position and the proper distance apart, others can nail on diagonals at the two ends, and, after all is square and plumb, the two string-pieces, A, E and C, G, may be securely nailed in place, and the rafter M, O nailed to M, N and O, P. This finishes the framework proper, for the club-house.

Passageway.

To make the frame for the underground hall or passageway, first nail Q, S across the door-jambs, to form the top to the doorway, after which put in the supports Q, R and S, T. Next build the frame U, V, X, W, and join it to Q, S

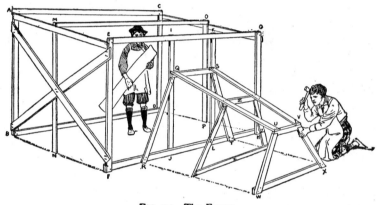

FIG. 77.—The Frame.

by the two pieces, Q, U and S, V, and put in the middle frame-support marked Z, Z, Z, Z.

The passageway should be about six feet feet long, and the front doorway (U, V, X, W, Fig. 80) of just sufficient size to enable you to creep through with comfort. The bottom-piece, W, X, can be nailed to a couple of stakes driven in the ground for that purpose. The next thing in order is the floor, and to make this firm you must lay a number of two-by-fours, parallel to B, D and F, H and see that they are level. You will need a number of shorter pieces of the same material, to run parallel to F, H and W, X for the hall floor, as may be seen in Fig. 79. Across these nail your floor securely, as shown in Fig. 79.

There Are No Windows

to the underground house, and but two openings: one in the roof for the ventilator, and the doorway, Q, S, L, J, Fig. 77. Since the outside of the wall of this sort of a house is hidden by earth, it is not necessary to remove the diagonal braces upon the ends or sides, but the inside should be neatly finished, and the four sides must be boarded up from the inside, after which the side-walls to the passage-way may be nailed on from the outside, the boards running from the floor to the string-pieces, Q, U and S V, as shown in Fig. 79. When this is finished, roof the house, laying the boards parallel with A, E and C, G, and allowing them to project front and rear and overlap at the sides. Over each crack in the roof nail another plank, as shown in Fig. 79.

The Roof

may be made without the overlapping boards and the cracks covered with strips of tar-paper or old oil-cloth, or the roof may be preserved and the cracks filled by treating the whole to a coating of hot tar, daubed on with a brush made from rags tied to the end of a stick. Any sort of roof which will keep out the rain will answer the purpose.

Gumption.

The plans given may be, and are expected to be, altered to suit requirements. If you use this roofing you must use substantial supports, in the way of rafters, and put them close together. In all cases, use your common-sense.

Don't put much earth on a frail roof ; it is only necessary to cover the boards with sufficient earth or sod to conceal the wood.

Make a long box, of four boards (Fig. 82), for

A Ventilator,

and set this over a square hole cut in the roof for this purpose. The ventilator should project at least one foot and a half above ground, and the top or vent be protected by wire-netting or cross-pieces, nailed on as shown in Fig. 82. Now spread small brush over the boards, and dry leaves or straw over the brush, then shovel the dirt back in the excavation until the club-house is entirely covered ; pack the soil firmly all around the house, leaving only the top of the ventilator and the front door uncovered.

FIGS. 79-83.—Cross-Section of House.

When all is finished to your satisfaction, conceal the ventilator by brush or transplanted weeds or shrubs, and scatter grass and clover-seed over the new earth. Make a strong door, after the plan in Fig. 81, and fasten it on the front entrance with good hinges and a padlock, and place some brush or growing shrubs in front of the door.

After the Grass Begins to Grow

there will be little to cause the passers-by to suspect that the green bank conceals a room well supplied with chess, checkers, boys' books, and everything to make a boy happy.

Dangerous Caves.

There is an impulse implanted in all boys, which impels them to dig caves in every convenient bank, and these caves are always more or less dangerous from their liability to cave in upon the youthful miners. It not infrequently occurs that sad accidents do happen to youngsters, who, on account of lack of instruction, attempt to make underground retreats in some sandy bank, by boring a hole in the face of the hill. If, however, they make an excavation as here directed, and illustrated by Figs. 76 and 76a, their parents need feel no apprehension, for there is no more liability to accident than if they were digging in the home garden. Many of these houses have already been constructed.

CHAPTER IX.

A BOYS' CLUB-HOUSE ON THE WATER.

WE cannot all be Robinson Crusoes, and real desert islands are scarce, but with a little work we can build artificial islands, upon which Robinson Crusoe cabins of novel designs may be erected, and by forming

Crusoe-Clubs,

consisting of as many members as the island homes will accommodate, we shall have plenty of company. The President of such a club may be called "Robinson Crusoe"; the Secretary, "Man Friday"; the Treasurer, "The Goat," and the Captain, "The Parrot." In selecting a site for the club-house, choose a bar or shallow place in some small lake or pond.

Not only is the

Foundation of the Club-House Submerged,

but it must be built under water, and every foot of water adds to the difficulties. The following plans are made for foundations to be laid in water not much over waist-deep. For the convenience of the draughtsman, the bottom in the diagrams is supposed to be level.

The Building Material

necessary is such as the lumber-pile, the farm-yard, wood-shed or forest will supply, and the necessary tools consist

of some mauls, a saw, auger, and hatchet. Make your
own mauls, by sawing off the ends of hardwood posts and
fitting handles in holes bored
in the pieces of hardwood for
that purpose. Fig. 84 shows
a boy using a home-made
maul.

Should you be so fortun-
ate as to be able to locate
your house over

FIG. 84.—Using a Home-made Maul.

A Soft Bottom,

make the corner piers by
driving a number of stakes
in a circle (Fig. 84), over
which slip a barrel (Fig. 85)
which has previously had both its heads removed. If you
have no barrels a box, similarly
treated, will answer the purpose, and in case you have no
boxes, cribs, made in the form of
boxes open at the top and bottom, may be used. Should you
be ambitious to build in

True Robinson Crusoe Style,

drive a number of long stakes
securely, in the form of a circle,
in the bottom of the pond, as

FIG. 85.—Placing the Barrel.

in Fig. 84, and then with grape-vines and other creepers
weave a basket (Fig. 86). "Crusoe" should know how to

do all these things. "The Parrot" should have charge of the transportation of material, and "The Goat" collect the lumber, cobblestones, stakes, and vines. All kinds of vines and creepers are good for basket-work, and almost any sort of stakes will answer, but "The Goat" must see that neither poison-sumac nor poison-ivy is used. Both of these plants must be avoided in any work of this kind, as they are extremely dangerous to comfort, and may cause an amount of irritation which will confine the victim to his bed for days.

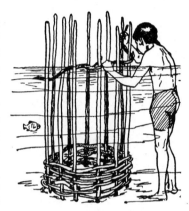

FIG. 86.—The Basket.

Where vines are scarce, almost any sort of green branches may be made to answer the purpose, willow being especially adapted for basket-work; but all the larger branches should be split in half to make them pliable enough to bend without breaking. You may now

Weave a Basket

by passing the vine alternately inside and outside of the stakes in the circle (Fig. 86), and when the end of the first piece in hand is reached you must duck your head under water and push the vine to the bottom of the stakes. Beginning where the last piece ended, weave a second piece of vine and push it down to the bottom, and so on until the top of the water is reached. It is great fun to make these cribs, and not at all difficult work, and when they are done and filled with cobblestones they make fine piers for a club-house or an artificial island.

The Foundation Posts

of the club-house should be four or five inches in diameter and sharpened at their lower ends, but even then you will probably find that the united strength of several boys is not sufficient to force them far enough into the bottom to

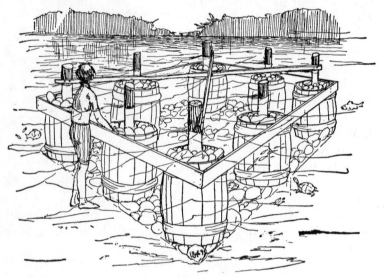

FIG. 87.—The Foundation.

prevent swaying.   Drive your foundation posts in the middle of the basket-crib and then

Fill the Crib with Stones.

When the cribs are full, as the barrels are in Fig. 87, they will form durable stone piers.   Four such piers will support a house big enough for from two to four boys.   In this case the foundation posts should be long enough to form the four corners of the house.   To make the posts steady, nail two diagonal binders on the posts, from corner to corner, crossing them in the centre (Fig. 87).

Let these diagonals be just above the water, and above these, and out of reach of waves, nail four

More Binders,

in the form of a square, as A, B, C, D, in Fig. 88 are arranged.   These form the support for the floor, and four

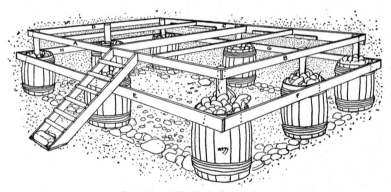

FIG. 88.—A Finished Foundation.

more at the top of the corner or foundation poles will make a support for the roof.   The rest of the work is simple ; it is only necessary to lay a floor, put on a roof, and to board up the sides to have as snug a cabin as boys need want in summer-time.   By using more piers you can make a foundation of any size.

When

The Bottom of the Pond

is hard sand, or stones, the basket-cribs may be built on shore in the same manner as described, but in this case it is neither necessary nor advisable to drive the stakes far into the earth. When finished the crib will hold together and may be removed from the land without dislocating the stakes, as the vines will hold them tightly in the structure.

You cannot possibly force your corner posts into the soil through hard sand or stones, and you must, therefore, be content to rest their lower ends upon the bottom, in which case make a stand for them by spiking two short boards, in the form of a cross, on the lower end of the posts, then slip your cribs over the posts (Fig. 89). While two boys hold the post and crib in place the others can fill the crib with cobble-stones, which will steady the post until it is made entirely secure by diagonal braces and the four binders, A, B, C, D. No

FIG. 89.—Barrel Cribs.

matter how uneven the ends of the posts may be at first, the top of the binders, A, B, C, D, must be exactly level.

The water, when calm, is

Always Level,

and if you measure three feet from its surface, and mark the point on each post, you can make the binders exactly level by nailing them with their top edge exactly even with the three-foot mark on the corner posts. The posts may now be sawed off even with the binders (Fig. 88) and the floor laid.

In a Large Building,

four extra binders nailed to the top of the crib (E, F, G, H, Fig. 88), will give finish to the structure, especially if they are floored over to the edge of the top floor, thus making a step at the surface or under the water. Stairs may be built, as shown in Fig. 88. On hard bottoms they are anchored at the lower end by a large stone placed upon a board, which joins the lower ends of the side-boards; but on soft bottoms the stairs may be first nailed to two stakes, which are afterward driven into the mud. Fig. 90 shows the platform finished, and skeleton house erected. To build this house place the two two-inch by four-inch strips, J, N and M, Q, on the platform at the required distance apart, and "toe-nail" them in place—driving the nails slantingly from the sides into the floor (Fig. 92).

Temporary diagonal Braces

may be used until you have your skeleton house far enough advanced to fit in some horizontal cross-pieces between the uprights, and to "toe-nail" them in place. Put in two sets of braces on

FIGS. 90-92.—Frame of House.

each side, one above and one below the window openings, and in the front frame, J, K, L, M, one over the pro-

posed doorway, and two more in the rear frame, N, O,
P, Q, the latter extending from the upright, N, O, to
the upright P, Q, and parallel to N, Q, as explained by
Fig. 91.   When these braces are in place your frame will
be stiff enough to nail on the sidings of slabs, boards or
poles, and after they are in position the roof may be put on
with no fear of the structure's falling.   The roof may be
made of boards, as described in the underground club-
house.

An Artificial Island

can be made, by erecting the corner cribs and bracing them,
as described for the club-house, and then packing brush,
loaded with stones, between the boundaries of the foundation.

Lay the brush with the stems pointing one way and
place stones on top, one layer of weighted brush over another, until you have reached a level two feet above the
water.   Cover the top brush with hay, straw, or old leaves,
and place a layer of sods over the leaves.

Upon this foundation you can place as much earth as
your industry will permit, and you will have a substantial
little island, upon which grass or plants will grow, and beneath which the little fishes can live amid the submerged
brush.

Moving in for the Summer.

CHAPTER X.

HOW TO HAVE FUN AT A PICNIC.

IF feasible take hammocks and ropes for swings along with you and don't forget a

"Joggling-Board."

This is a very popular invention, from South Carolina, and consists of a pine or hemlock plank, one inch thick, one

The Joggling Board.

foot wide and ten feet long, which, when supported at each end by solid supports, or ropes from the limb of a tree, forms a seat which responds to every movement of the person sitting in the centre, with a gentle, delightful joggle.

If you use a wagon, stage, or omnibus, to reach the picnic ground, start a game of

Turnpike Loo.

First divide your party into two sides, the lefts and the rights, including the driver.   Each side names and counts all animals passed upon their respective sides—a dog, cat, sheep, pig, cow, horse, or domestic fowl, each counts one ; a man, woman or child, five ; an animal with a bell, fifteen ; an animal looking out of a barn or stable window, twenty ; and a dog, cat, or baby in a farm-house window counts fifty ; the game is two hundred.

The Driver

will endeavor to pass all animals upon his side; but the leader of the left will get out at times and thwart the driver, by chasing and coaxing the creatures to his side.   The game is exciting, producing much mirth for the picnickers and amazement among the farmers and live-stock.

A great improvement upon the old-fashioned hamper of heavy dishes is the

Modern Pasteboard Box,

cheap wooden pie-plates, and paper napkins.   Wrap your sandwiches in a damp linen napkin and with an outside wrapper of confectioners' paraffine paper and pack them, and everything else you can, in pasteboard boxes.   Salads and similar foods may be carried in wide-mouthed glass jars; mayonnaise dressing, sliced cucumbers and tomatoes in the same manner.

Pack the Ground Coffee,

with an egg rolled in paper, in the coffee-pot. Make the egg into a bundle large enough to fit on top the coffee, with no room to roll or jolt about. The butter or other grease, left after the feast, may be melted and poured into the small paper or wooden boxes; a wick of twisted paper or rag, thoroughly soaked with the grease, will make a lamp. Name the lamps, set them afloat, and the light which goes out last is supposed to be your truest admirer.

The Rhode Island Clam-Bake,

the Pennsylvania Pond-Stew, the Virginia Soup, and the Kentucky Burgoo, are about the jolliest forms of picnics known in this country.

Resting in the laps of the high hills and mountains of Pennsylvania are many small lakes. Here the picnickers spend the forenoon capturing what edible aquatic creatures their skill can procure, all of which are put into the stew-pan along with vegetables, thus making a sort of fresh-water chowder of the most appetizing nature.

Burgoo.

In Virginia and Kentucky it was an old-time custom for the gentlemen to spend the forenoon hunting and fishing, and the slaves in the afternoon cooked the game and fish in great iron pots, hung over blazing wood fires, thus making a most savory dish for the ladies who joined the party toward evening. This is the origin of the Virginia Soup and the Kentucky Burgoo.

The latter is the most famous, and has been enjoyed by

all great Kentuckians, from Marshall, Clay, and Lincoln, to the present day.

Since the practical extermination of game, domestic fowls are used as a substitute for wild birds. When you have a Burgoo ask a certain number of guests to each bring a raw

The Burgoo.

dressed chicken, duck, or goose, and others to bring vege-tables, peeled and ready for the pot. The head cook, or Burgoo-Master, brings herbs, salt, freshly ground black pep-per, salt pork, olives, and lemons.

As a substitute for the old-fashioned, cumbersome iron kettle, take a large, pail-shaped

Clothes-boiler,

bought new for the occasion. Build your fire between two green logs, and use the logs to support the boiler over the flames. Half fill the boiler with water and pour in all the vegetables and meats, and allow them to boil slowly until the bones settle to the bottom and the other ingredients are reduced to a pulp.

It Takes Time to Properly Cook a Burgoo,

and the contents of the pot must be constantly stirred, especially when nearly cooked, in order to prevent the vegetables and meat from burning and imparting a scorched flavor to the soup.

The stirring is done with long-handled paddles, crudely whittled by the men. The young people who take turns in stirring, walk around the steaming caldron to the time of vocal music, and should any maid, by accident or design, click her paddle against one in the hands of a young man, the young man may claim a penalty.

When the Soup is Cooked

it is seasoned to taste, and must be served hot. The olives are extracted from the olive jar, and one olive placed in each cup, with a slice of lemon. The olive liquid remaining in the jar is poured into the hot soup and then the soup is ladled out and poured over the lemon and olive in each cup. If the Burgoo-Master has attended strictly to his work the picnickers will find it one of the most delicious soups which they have ever tasted.

The preparation of the Burgoo does not employ all hands of a large party all the time, and the idle ones may amuse themselves with

A Game of Jack-Fagots.

An armful of fagots is held a foot from the ground and allowed to fall, and then the first player, with a crooked

stick, hooks out as many fagots as possible, without disturbing the remainder. The slightest movement of a fagot, not hooked, ends the turn, and, after counting the score, the fagots are bunched and allowed to fall for the next player. The sticks successfully removed by each player constitute the individual scores.

Jack Fagots.

In the afternoon all must join in some games—little folks, old folks, and young folks. Choose some of the games children play, such as

Old Dan Tucker.

By lot, or by old-fashioned counting out verses, let chance decide who is to be "It," or Tucker, and let all the other males, big and little, select partners as they would for a dance, and form a ring around Tucker. At

a signal from " It " each player must face his partner and
sing

> " Hipperty-Hop, Hipperty-Hop !
> Joyfully now we sing,
> As we hop to the right and hop to the left,
> Around Dan Tucker's ring ! "

Keeping time with the music the players go, with a
hipperty-hop step, to the right of the first and to the left of
the second, weaving in and out until the partners meet;
then right-about-face and back again in the same manner
to their places.   Next all join hands and

Circle Around Tucker, Singing

> " Go round and round old Tucker,
> Go round and round old Tucker,
> Go round and round old Tucker,
> As we have gone before ! "

When the couples are again back in their places the
song is changed, and suiting the action to

The Words, They Sing

> " I put my right hand in,
> I put my left hand out,
> I give my right hand a shake, shake, shake,
> And turn myself about ! "

Using the same verse the girls now sing, " I put my
pretty face in," etc.   Then their partners sing, " I put my
'ugly mug' in," etc.   Then all sing " I put my right foot in,"
etc., and after the last shake of the right foot all again join
hands and advancing and

Crowding on Tucker

from all sides, and back again to places, they sing

" Go in and out the window,
Go in and out the window,
Go in and out the window,
As we have done before."

Changing the refrain, they next sing

"Go Stand and Face Your Partner,"

repeating three times, and ending with "as we have done before." At the last word they face their partners and give them their right hand, their left hand to the next, and, giving hands right and left, sing "Hipperty-Hop Hipperty-Hop," ending this time with

"Now Let Old Tucker Join Us."

As soon as Tucker has secured the partner he wants he shouts

" Get out of the way for old Dan Tucker,
You're too late to get your supper,"

and the boy or man left without a partner is "It" for the next game. The tunes for the verses can be obtained from the children. This is all taken from children's games.

Pitch-peg-pin Pitching

is a great game for hilarious fun. The pegs are sticks, two feet long, sharpened at one end, and nine in number. Put the pointed ends in the ground, forming a diamond, with each peg two feet from its nearest neighbor, and the one at one apex about twenty feet from a taw-line.

Let All the Girls,

big, little, married, and unmarried, form one side, and an equal number of boys, old and young, form the other side. The boys then choose a First Lady, who is to lead their opponents, and the girls choose a First Gentleman, who is to command the men. With three short clubs in her hands the First Lady toes the taw-line and endeavors to knock all the pegs down, in three consecutive throws with the clubs.

The pegs are then reset, the score recorded, and

The First Gentleman Takes

the clubs and his turn. When all have had a turn the individual scores are compared, and the right arm of each man or boy is bound with a pocket-handkerchief to the left arm of the girl, woman or matron whose score most nearly approaches his own, and the First Lady and First Gentleman choose up for sides, taking a couple at each choice. In the order of their score number, the couples now take their turn pitching clubs at the pins, the man, of necessity, using his left hand and the woman her right to throw the clubs, which they do simultaneously.

The Scores

are again compared and the couples bound into fours, and the fours into sixes, until each side is bound into a continuous line, with only the left hand of the end man and the right hand of the end woman to pitch-peg-pin with, and make the final score of the game.

Lawn Hab-enihan.

Mark with a whitewash brush upon the grass, scratch with a stick upon the bare ground or hard sand of a shore, twelve concentric circles. Number the rings from the outside to the centre.

Supply each player with a dozen smooth stones, about the size of the palm of one's hand. If you can get flat, water-washed stones, with rounded edges, they make the best "Habs." Standing upon the taw-line at the distance from the target agreed upon, each player in turn pitches a hab at the target, or "Enihan," leaving a stone inside the circle struck. But if his hab rests upon a line which bounds the rings he loses his turn after the first shot. The player may remove a hab from the circle last struck, or set another hab in it, or, counting from where any one of his habs rests, can move that hab as many circles toward the centre as corresponds with the number of the circle last struck.

If this moves the hab to the centre and leaves some figures over he can place a new hab forward as many rings as correspond with the numbers left over. If any player can cast two habs into a circle occupied by some other player's hab, the successful player captures the other hab and removes it. The game consists of any specified number of points, and when any one of the players has no habs on the enihan the game is ended. Then each player counts the number of his habs in the centre and the number of captured habs, and whoever has the most adds to his or her individual score the number of habs left on the enihan. The players have three objects constantly in view: to protect his or her habs from capture by getting more than one in the same circle, to work to the centre, and to capture the opponent's habs. This is an exciting outdoor game, which may be played with the material at hand, and when two players have each a hab in the same circle, and each hab is moving nearer and nearer the centre, the danger of a lucky shot and capture keeps them " guessing."

CHAPTER XI.

HOW TO BUILD AND HOW TO FURNISH A DANIEL BOONE CABIN.

IMAGINATION is a great thing and can do wonders; it can surround the most commonplace objects with an atmosphere of romance, in which nothing is impossible or improbable. A whiff of smoke from the fireplace where wood is burning, means nothing but a faulty chimney; yet, as the smell of burning wood reaches the nostrils, Association sets the wheels of

Imagination's Mill

whirring, and all unbidden come visions floating through our minds of camps, camp-fires, fish—pickerel, bass, and trout; quail, rabbits, and venison-steaks, broiling over the hot coals. My, it makes a fellow hungry to think of such good things! Roasted ears of sweet-corn, flapjacks, and corn-dodgers, " piping hot," pass in a procession before us, and, as the sparks fly up the chimney,

The Ghosts of the Fireplace

troop in: and a hale and husky lot of ghosts they are, with their coon-skin caps, buckskin clothes, and beaded moccasins. Each ghost wears a strap slung over his shoulder, from which hang a bullet-pouch and a curiously engraved cow-horn powder-flask; as they file by, with their long single-barrelled flint-lock rifles, we are not surprised to see among them the great Daniel Boone, his friend Simon Kenton, and the unique, dashing, Davy Crockett.

All in vain do the trucks thunder by our windows, and futile are the efforts of the clanging cable-car bells and the roar of the great city to recall us to the present humdrum

Home of Young Pioneers.

times. We are under the spell of the king of magicians, and our minds are wandering free in the wild woods; we can even hear the distant wolves howl, and the blood curdling yell of the painted savage. Is it a wonder that we love the generous old-fashioned fireplace? Is it strange that the log-cabin is dear to the hearts of American boys?

The Log-House

saw the birth of our nation; its rude interior sheltered our great men, and beneath its slabbed roof heroes were born. To-day it is still the most practicable, durable, and simply constructed house invented for a forest home, and any boy can build a log-house large enough to form a comfortable camp for vacation days. For muscles unaccustomed to such exercise it is hard work to cut down large trees, and, unless the young woodsman has served an apprenticeship on a farm or in a lumber-camp, it is dangerous work to fell big timber; but any lad may cut down

Trees of a Smaller Growth,

without danger to life or limb. Small-sized logs save much labor in chopping, sawing, rolling, and "snaking" to camp; besides all this, logs of small diameter look best for a house of small dimensions.

Therefore, in selecting the material for your proposed house, choose only such trees as are best suited to the strength of the builders. There is no rule which fixes the diameter of a log or pole, so a log-house is a log-house, no matter whether the diameter of the log from which it is built be four inches or four feet. When a log is hauled by men, horses, or oxen, through the woods, it is called "snaking."

The "Skid"

is two or more logs laid on the ground, upon and across which the other logs are piled up for use. Common-sense will direct you to select only the timber which comes near-est being straight, and also to cut the logs considerably longer than the length marked on the plan.

Happy Days.

Fig. 93 shows the plan of a simple cabin, 6 feet wide by 10 feet long, inside measurement.

Fig. 95 is a rough sketch and plan of two such cabins under one roof, with a hallway, or "gallery," as they call it in the South, between them. Fig. 96 is a plan of the saddle-bag. In this sketch you will see how your house may be

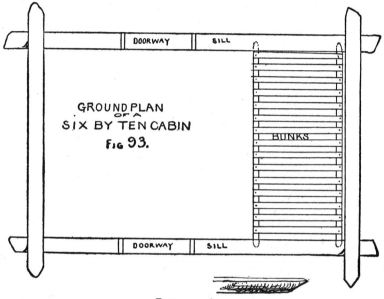

FIGS. 93 and 94.

enlarged, at any time, by the addition of a duplicate house, with a roofed space between the two.

First decide upon the exact spot where you intend to

Locate Your Cabin,

then stake out the cabin according to your plans, and clear the ground for the house.

To facilitate rolling the logs as you need them, arrange some skids close by the site of the house, and allow them to slant toward the proposed cabin.

If there are any stones handy,

Build a Foundation

by making a pile of stones a foot or two high, at each of the four corners, in such a manner that the logs resting on these supports will be at the same level at each end, level with each other, and exactly six feet apart.

For Floor-Joists

take a number of strong poles, and, with a sharp hatchet, give them a flat side for the floor-boards to rest upon, and trim off each end, wedge-shaped, as shown by Fig. 94, the rough sketch at the bottom right-hand corner of Fig. 93.

You understand, of course, that

The Floor-Supports

must be of sufficient length to reach from the front sill-log to the back sill-log.   Nail each joist at each end to the sill-

FIGS. 95 and 96.

logs, and place them about two feet apart. If it is thought that the flooring of the cabin makes too much work, you may build one with a "mud-sill," by using the hard earth for floor and foundation. Abraham Lincoln lived in a " mud-sill " house, and there are hundreds of such houses in the Southern States.

With the exception of the sill-logs, all the logs are notched at both ends and on both sides (Figs. 97 and 98); the sill-logs are notched at both ends, but only on one side, as shown by Fig. 98. Logs of the same diameter as the sill-logs can be laid between them on the bare ground and used for joists, but the best plan is a stone foundation, and a plank floor at least a foot or two above the earth.

Log-Rolling.

Now is the time to invite all your friends to a grand old-time log-rolling; ask the girls to come and cook the coffee and make the sandwiches.

The two end-logs may first be rolled down from the skids, notched and fitted in place across the ends of sill-logs (Fig. 93), and then the next two side-logs, and so on, alternating until the walls are built; but you must remember to allow for the doors, windows, and fireplace openings. When the walls are so high that it is a difficult task to lift the logs in position, put up a couple of skids and roll the logs up the incline, which is better than wasting your strength in trying to lift such burdens. When the walls have reached the height of the top of the lowest opening, nail some

Door and Window Opening

planks, temporarily, close to the proposed opening on both sides of it, and on the inside and outside of the house; this is to hold the logs in position while the opening is being cut. A, in Fig. 99, shows a binder. After the binders are in place, saw the top log through at the proposed opening, to allow room for the saw, and then proceed to build as before. See Fig. 98, showing opening over door and window ; the binders are not shown in this diagram.

A Fireplace

is by no means an absolute necessity for a summer cabin, but an open fire is a great addition to a house, and upon cool evenings, even in the summer-time, its genial warmth

THIS IS THE WAY TO NOTCH AND JOIN THE LOGS

FIGS. 97 and 98.

is not to be despised. The protruding ends of the logs, at the four corners of the cabin, may be left as they happen to be until the house is finished, no matter how irregular their appearance. With a two-handled saw, and a boy at each end, the ends may be cut off evenly ; this will give a finished appearance to the cabin. You can have

Any Sort of a Roof

which suits your fancy ; it may be framed, as described in Chapter VII., or, by using round poles, it may be framed as shown by Fig. 98 and roofed with slabs or planks, as shown by Fig. 100, or the roof may be shingled with "clap-boards," a name used for shingles or boards, about three feet long, and laid on as ordinary shingles are—first course at the eaves, second course breaking joints and overlapping the first, and so on, until the roof-tree is reached.

If shingles, clapboards, and planks are out of reach, the roof may be shingled with bark; if birch bark is used, it can be held in place by poles laid upon the outside of the roof, as I have often seen the hand-rived clapboards held in place where they use no nails in the construction of their homes.

The Most Essential Piece of Furniture

for the house, if you are to live in it, is the bed or bunk. This can be made in various simple and effective pat-terns. At the Sportsmen's Show in New York there was an elaborately constructed bedstead, made of the rough branches of trees, but however ornamental this style of couch may be, it is not essential to comfort, and requires time and skill to manufacture, neither of which the average boy is willing to lavish on camp furniture.

The Bunks

shown in the plan (Fig. 93), are made with two horizontal poles, flattened at the ends and upon one side, after the manner of the rough sketch at the Fig. 94. These poles extend from side to side of the cabin, and rest upon the logs of the wall, to which they are securely nailed. The ends are further supported by a cross-plank, or pole, fastened to the walls, as a support for the side-rods of the bunk.

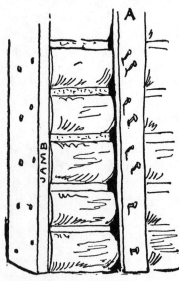

Slats are made of sticks split in half and nailed to the side-bars, as shown in the plan. One bunk is placed over another, until there is no room for more, and then the three or more bunks are filled with straw, hay, or spruce boughs, over which the blankets are spread, and the bed is made.

With a mud-sill house you can

FIG. 99.—Binder and Jamb for Opening.

Make a Lincoln Bed.

Abraham Lincoln's father had no bedstead, and no means of getting one but to make it, and no tools but an auger and axe to make it with. A stake was driven in the ground, near the corner of the cabin, about four feet from one of the walls, and six feet from the other. Auger-holes were then bored in the wall opposite, and poles driven into them, the other ends meeting on the stake; across these were laid laths rived from an oak, and upon them rested the straw-bed of our great President.

When Your House is Crowded,

the floor offers space for sleepers, and you may "choose up," for first choice. As a rule the top berth is first choice, as in it you feel less cramped for breathing-space, for there is nothing but the roof above you. Unless the boys are more than usually expert builders, there will be no lack of fresh air, even when your house is crowded. To prevent too much wind entering, it is well to

Stuff all the Spaces Between the Logs

with mud or clay, mixed with moss, and while some of the boys are in the woods gathering the moss, and others mix. ing and dampening the clay, the more skilled mechanics can

Make the Door

and hang it in the doorway, which, with the other proposed openings, may be now sawed out and heavy jambs nailed on, before the binders are removed. The wooden hinge of the door can be made of ash, hickory, or oak, and may be simply a straight stick or rod about six and a half feet long and two inches in diameter (Fig. 105). Bore a hole in the upper log over the doorway, about six inches deep; if the log is of less diameter than this, bore the hole through the log. Bore a hole in the lower, or sill-log, but make it only deep enough to securely hold one end of your hinge-rod, and then trim the rod to fit in this hole, making it a trifle shorter than the distance between the end of the top hole and the end of the sill hole. Flatten one side of the hinge-rod, so that it may fit neatly along the edge of the door, but do not fasten it on the door until after the rod is in place. Spring the rod in place by slipping the top end into the top hole as far as it will go, and then pushing the bottom end over the sill hole. When it slips in place set the door up, in the position it would be when wide open and fasten it to the flattened edge of the hinge-rod, with good strong screws. Close the door and mark the edge on the jamb, then nail a narrow strip of wood along the line, to prevent the door swinging any farther than it is necessary for it to swing when closed ; or make it as shown by Fig. 105, and hang it with iron hinges, as doors at home are hung.

FIG. 100.—Board or Slab Roof.

If You Have Money to Spend,

and men to work under your directions, you can have the regulation door, floor, and roof; the cracks in the wall calked with mortar, and a stone or brick chimney and fireplace built. In fact, you can make a palace of logs, with plate-glass windows, but *you will not have a log-cabin, and you will miss all the fun to be derived from creating something by your own labor,* which is the highest sort of joy—the joy of the artist! Any "chump," with money, can hire men to build houses which would be impossible for his stupid brain and clumsy hands to accomplish. Besides which, the men he hired to do the work would be the only ones who derived any real pleasure from the construction of the houses.

You must not understand from this that you are to use

Oiled Paper for Glass, in Your Windows,

if you can obtain real glass, but that in case you cannot, the paper makes a good substitute, and one which was used in many a pioneer's cabin. In Virginia there are log-houses, still occupied, which have not even a paper window—a hole, closed in bad weather by a wooden shutter, being the only opening besides the doors, and the moonshiners of the mountain districts seldom have windows at all, but depend upon a front and rear door to supply light for the house, and when these doors are closed the fire supplies the illumination.

The Lamps

they use, when they have any, are small pans or saucers filled with melted fat, in which a piece of rag is placed, and furnishes a wick for this primitive light. In 1897 I was given one of these "Betty lights" by a mountain host, to light me to bed.

Every boy's log-house should be supplied with lanterns and candles, but the candles must be stored in tin boxes, otherwise

The Brownies Will Eat Them.

Brownies are the wild wood-mice and flying-squirrels which will use your house during your absence, and not only

eat the candles, but anything else you may leave unprotected.   They ate up my soap, and then, for dessert, went
to the kitchen and ate up the stove-polish.   In small houses
you will probably not have stove-polish, or stoves.

After the opening in the wall of the cabin for the fireplace is sawed out, you may build up a good, strong wall, on
the three outer sides of

The Fireplace

(Figs. 106 and 107).   Build these walls as you did the cabin
walls, and fit the ends of the logs neatly against the cabin
logs, and put " chunks " in between the logs at the cabin end,
to level them.   When the walls are as high as the opening
in the cabin, you are ready to begin the work of building
the inside clay-lining.

It will take a considerable quantity of clay to finish your
fireplace and chimney, and a rough box, like the mortar-box
used by builders, will be found most convenient for mixing
the clay.

Saw off the ends of some sticks of wood and make some

Wooden Hammers, or Mauls,

of them, by boring holes through the pieces you have sawed
off and putting handles in the holes.   These mauls may vary
from three to five inches in diameter, and will be found to
be the most convenient sort of tool for breaking the dry
clay before it is dampened, and they will also be of great
service in beating the clay down, for the fireplace and hearth.
Make the floor to the fireplace and the hearth by spreading
the damp clay over the space and hammering it down until
it is hard ; add more clay, and beat it until the hearth and
fire-floor (Figs. 107 and 108) are level and firm.   You may
then put on enough water to make the surface slippery, and

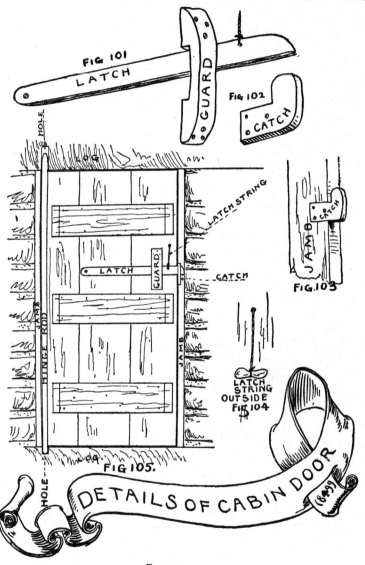

FIG 101
LATCH

GUARD

FIG 102
CATCH

HOLE

LOG

LATCH STRING

LATCH

GUARD

CATCH

CATCH

JAMB

FIG.103

JAMB

HINGE ROD

JAMB

LATCH
STRING
OUTSIDE
FIG 104

FIG 105.

HOLE

DETAILS OF CABIN DOOR

FIGS. 101-105.

smooth it off with a trowel made of a shingle and a branch, after the manner of the one shown in the foreground of Fig. 98.

Next Build Your Clay Walls

on the inside, against the log outside walls, and extending to the inside of the cabin wall. Make the clay into the form of bricks and build up the jambs and lining, about one foot thick, to the top of the fireplace, using wet clay for mortar.

For the Chimney

split some sticks and make them about one inch wide by one and one-half inch thick, and with clay for mortar build the

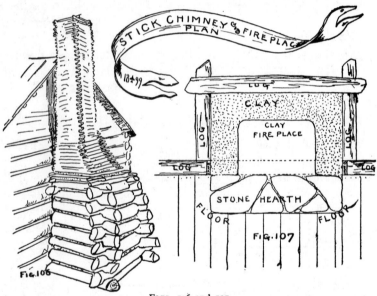

FIGS. 106 and 107.

chimney, log-cabin style (Fig. 106), to the required height, leaving a space between the chimney and outside wall of the house. Plaster it well with clay, especially upon the inside, and be careful to keep it plumb.

A short time ago, while on a sketching trip through the mountains of East Tennessee and Kentucky, I saw hundreds of these

Stick Chimneys

which have done service for years. Some of them were beautiful specimens of skill, while others had a decided list to port or starboard, as a sailor would say, and were apparently carelessly made.

In the mountains the fireplaces are lined with stones, in place of clay, but in Illinois, where stones are scarce and mud plenty, the old-time log-cabin hearth and fireplace were always made of clay.

Besides the berths or bunks already described, a table and some benches, or three-legged stools, will be found very useful articles of furniture. In a small house a

Table Takes Up Needed Room,

and as it is principally used at meal-time, a contrivance that may be put away when not in use is most desirable; such a table can be made of two wooden horses, with boards laid across them. When the weather is fair the table may be set out-doors, and when the weather is foul it can be placed in-doors. The horses and boards may be kept on the porch, if you have one, or in a shed or on the rafters overhead.

Three-Legged Stools.

A piece of two-inch plank, with three oak, ash, or hickory sticks driven into three holes bored for the purpose, makes a stool which will last a lifetime. Two such stools have been in use for twelve or thirteen years in my Pike County (Pa.) cabin, and are just as good as new to-day.

Now, when your work is done and you balance yourself on a three-legged stool, and rest from your labors, remember you are sitting on what has before now proved to be the incipient Presidential chair.

General Camp Notes for Old Boys.

If the boys suppose that their parents are not interested in out-door life, they are mistaken, for the author never fails to receive a batch of letters from grown-up people, whenever he publishes an out-door article for the boys. That the boys may answer the questions put to the author by the parents, and incidentally profit themselves by the information, the following suggestions to campers are given.

It will be observed that, when talking to the old people, the question of having sufficient funds is not taken as strictly into account as it is in all the plans for the boys themselves.

When You Start for Camp

leave artificialities and fripperies behind, packed up in camphor, and bring only your free, untrammelled self with you, and ho! for a frolic, for flapjacks and coffee, sweet-scented spruce boughs, camp-fires, and the fireside song, and the music of the banjo. Let your first care be to secure cheerful, happy companions, as the most important articles for your camping outfit.

White flannel trousers and blazers are for the seaside and summer resorts, not for camp. You go to camp for health and fun, not for display; therefore leave your good clothes in your trunk at the last railroad station, to be called for when you quit the woods and once more enter the land of creased trousers and starched shirts, of stocks, long skirts, and ties.

How the Women Should Dress.

A woman's camp-dress should consist of a scant, short skirt, bloomers, leggings, and stout, broad-soled shoes, loose shirt-waist, and Norfolk jacket, the latter plentifully supplied with pockets. Whatever prejudice a woman may have against short skirts and bloomers is soon overcome after she has tried to climb fallen trees and rocks, or made her way through thick underbrush, encumbered with the absurd long skirts of the house or street, or after she has tramped to camp with a wet and bedrabbled skirt flapping around her ankles, caused by a walk in the dewy morning, or a paddle in a leaky boat. Women should have their dresses made of strong material, with "lots of pockets," like a man's hunting-clothes. They will find their capabilities for enjoyment greatly enhanced by this, and the men, at least, will think them just as bewitching and far better companions than they would be if they were dressed in city gowns, hats and feathers, and low shoes.

The Requirements for a Camp.

Each person in camp should be supplied with a good, big-bladed jack-knife; a woodsman, or, what is about the same thing, a person with good common-sense, can supply himself with food and shelter, with no other ready-made tool than a good strong knife.

Salt, pepper, and sugar, must be put on the list; then flour in sack, oatmeal, cornmeal, rice, and lard; crackers, beans, coffee in tin, tea in bag, cocoa, condensed milk in cans, evaporated cream in cans, butter in pail, pickles, dried fruit in bags, a bag of potatoes, molasses, pork, boneless bacon, and, if you are fond of it, a few jars of orange marmalade; sal-soda for sweetening "dubs," and ginger for medicinal purposes; several cakes of common soap for dish-washing, some dish-towels, and some soap for toilet purposes; also a tin coffee-pot, a long-handled frying-pan, a small griddle, a nest of tin pails, the smallest capable of holding a quart or less, and the largest a gallon or more; two or three paper pails or water-buckets, two or three iron kitchen spoons and forks, and a camp boiler, a firkin and a wooden spoon, also a strong axe and a hatchet.

From the Stand-point of Health.

It is presupposed that people who intend to spend their vacation in camp are lovers of the beautiful; consequently, in selecting a camping-place, a spot should be chosen which gives the finest possible view of mountains, lakes, or rivers, even if some inconvenience must be suffered in the selection. The camp must be dry and well-drained, so that in case of sudden storms there will be no danger of the water flooding the tents, wetting the bedding or spoiling the food. A gentle sloping ground is best. Avoid locating in the track or below the mouths of innocent-looking gullies or ravines, that may, in case of rain, be developed into torrents of muddy water, and sweep the camp like a cloud-burst.

A supply of pure water contributes as much to the enjoyment of the campers as to the preservation of health. Common-sense will direct that the camp be selected within easy reach of some bubbling spring or fresh, uncontaminated brook of running water, but there is another thing of paramount importance, and that is a handy supply of fuel. The latter is of even more importance than that of

water. With a wooden man-yoke, water is easily transported for quite a distance, but no one who has not tried
it can realize the difficulty of carrying fuel even a short
distance.

Making the Shack or Shelter.

The Adirondack camp is made from the materials furnished by the forest, and it is put together in the form of a
shack or shelter, by the woodsmen or guides. Spruce-trees,
eight or nine inches in diameter, are cut down, quickly
stripped of their bark, and one of them suspended between
two trees eight or ten feet from the ground, or is supported by forked sticks. Others are then laid standing up to
it, and the incline is shingled with the bark, to keep out the
rain. Your bed is on the ground beneath the bark roof.
Put a log at the head, and a smaller one at the foot, and
cover the intervening space with a thick layer of flat spruce
boughs, neatly laid, with all the unnecessary sticks thrown
out; chop down some young balsams and strip them of all
their twigs; selecting all those of about twelve inches in
length, begin at the foot of the bed and work up, sticking
the butt-ends of the balsam twigs into the spruce boughs.
Place them as close together as possible, with their tops
slightly inclining to the foot of the couch. After all the
balsam is planted scatter the fine tips of some hemlock
boughs over the balsam, and spread your blanket over all.
Any bag or pillow-case, filled with hemlock and balsam tips,
makes a good, sweet-scented pillow. All that then remains
to be done is to fill up the ends of the shack with brush,
roll a back-log in front of your camp, and start the fire.
At night spread your blankets on the spruce twigs, stretch
yourself out and watch the dying embers of the fire until
you gradually drift into the sweet slumber of the camper.

The Brush-Covered Lean-to

is a triangular tent, open in front, made of one piece of canvas fastened to a horizontal pole in front, to the ground in the rear, and hanging down at the sides. Over this a rude, shack-like Adirondack camp is built, not to keep out rain but to protect the canvas, with the green brush, from sparks from the camp-fire. In no case must the brush touch the cloth, for during a rain the canvas will leak wherever any object is resting against it, either from the inside or outside.

A tent is the favorite abode of all campers. They are transported with much greater ease than the most simply-constructed portable house. A tent may be erected with the expenditure of less labor than any of the preceding camps, and furnishes a comfortable shelter all the year round. Even in the bleak mountains of Alaska tents are often used by miners, wintering near their mines. A good wall-tent, with a fly and a wooden floor, is protection enough for the most delicate of persons.

Standard drills and yacht twills are better adapted to the camper's purposes than heavier materials, and besides are less expensive. The list prices of wall-tents, from nine by nine feet to sixteen and a half by fourteen feet, are from $14 to $26. The flies are listed at from $4.50 to $9.70.

In Tents with Roofed Verandas.

The Amazon tents are in the form of a lean-to, with a roofed veranda, so to speak, in front.

Shanties are small houses of plank, roofed with plank, and are built by the natives, at costs varying with the price and accessibility of the lumber. A good, water-tight shanty ought to be erected in most sections for about $25. Bunks of planks are built in the shanties, one above the other, and, when filled with straw and covered with a blanket, make comfortable sleeping-quarters.

Portable houses are now manufactured of all forms and sizes, from a child's small playhouse to a two-story frame store. These buildings are made in sections; all parts are numbered and labelled, and may be put together and taken apart at will. Many of these houses are designed especially for camps, and may be shipped to the camping-ground with little trouble and erected with little loss of time. At the same factory may be purchased terra-cotta chimneys, in sections, ready to be stacked up for use. Some people prefer to build a chimney of stone or brick and leave it standing when the house is moved, others making stovepipe serve for a chimney.

What is Needed for Table and Larder.

For table furniture select white blue-rimmed cups and saucers, and plates of granite-ware. The gray enamelled ware is not as good, for many reasons. These enamelled or granite-ware dishes are as easily cleaned as china, but, unlike china, they will not break. Nickel-plated teaspoons are in every way as good as silver for camp purposes, and should not cost more than three cents apiece. Knives and forks to match can easily be found. Be sure they are modern ones with three tines.

FIG. 108.

Lay in a supply of candles, and two or three common stable lanterns. You may add to these items as many luxuries as your baggage will supply room for, or your purse or taste dictate. Fruit syrups, such as are used at reputable soda-water fountains, make very pleasant and healthful drinks when combined with good, cold spring-water. Lemons will keep in a cool, dry place for two weeks, and as a garnish for fish or soup not only give an appetizing look, which, as a rule, is unnecessary in camp food, but they add to the taste and relish, which is a property that persons blessed with good appetites appreciate, even when on a camping expedition.

CHAPTER XII.

A FLAT-BOATMAN'S HORN.

IT was in the golden age of whittling that wooden bugles and the Wabash horns were in their prime.

It is hardly an exaggerated figure of speech to say that the United States, with all its power and wealth, has been whittled out of the raw material by our ancestors, with their Barlow knives.

I think I have already told the readers, in one of my other books, that the practice of

Whittling

was not formerly confined to the youth of the country; lawyers, merchants, and statesmen, were adepts in the art, and on the counter of every well-regulated tavern was always to be found a heap of sweet-smelling cedar sticks for the guests to whittle, after meals.

Even as early as Puritan times the jack-knives were busy, and the little conscience-stricken Nathaniel Mathers confesses that " of the manifold sins which then I was guilty of none so sticks upon me as that, being very young, I was *whittling on the Sabbath day*, and for fear of being seen I did it behind the door."

Times have changed since this poor little chap hid behind the door to whittle a stick, and some of the less conscientious descendants of the Puritans would not dare now to whittle on Sunday, or any other day, for fear of cutting their clumsy, untrained fingers. But the fingers of the readers of this book, I trust, are skilful in the use of a pocket-knife, and for them it will not be a difficult task to make a Wabash, or Flat-boatman's, wooden horn.

The wooden horn was the particular favorite of the jolly, reckless flat-boatmen. Its soft musical notes sounded especially sweet and mellow in the early morning, when the boatmen were casting loose their cables from their moorings. From Pittsburg to New Orleans the reveille of the boatmen's horns announced the dawn of another day.

Descriptions of these horns have come to us from our pioneer grandparents, and printed accounts can only be found by rummaging among old Western papers. The Frankfort (Kentucky) *Commonwealth*, in 1836, published some verses extolling the boatman's music:

> Oh, boatman, wind that horn again!
>   For never did the joyous air
>   Upon its lambent bosom bear
> So wild, so soft, so sweet a strain.

And this horn was made of the same material as the boat. They performed upon a wooden bugle of long conical shape, constructed of small wooden staves, which, according to all accounts, produced sounds of a wonderfully sweet tone. On a beautiful, clear and still morning the echoes of the boatmen's trumpets, prolonged at a great distance through the neighboring woods and hills which bordered the river, are said to have possessed a charm and enchantment which none can realize but those who have heard them.

The Western boatmen were not the only ones who used

Wooden Bugles,

for there is an instrument of this kind still preserved in Kentucky, and is now, or was a few years ago, in the posses-

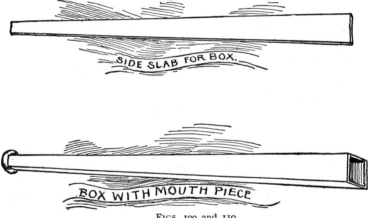

SIDE SLAB FOR BOX.

BOX WITH MOUTH PIECE

FIGS. 109 and 110.

sion of Mrs. Annie Mayhall, a granddaughter of Captain Robert Collins.

Colonel Richard Johnson made a famous charge in the war of 1812, and Captain Bob Collins sounded the charge on his home-made cedar horn.

If there are any illustrations of this charge, the bugler will no doubt be represented as blowing on the regulation brass instrument; but you must remember, boys, that the

artists were not in that fight.   Artists have a way of doing
things up fine, as may be seen by the pictures of our

FIG. III.

Revolutionary Soldiers,

all in regulation uniforms, when
the truth is that there was scarcely
a uniformed regiment in the army.
The grand old fellows fought in
their hunting garb, or the dress
they wore on the farm, in the
store, the church, or the tavern;
and while they may not have used
wooden horns, it is very probable
that many a Continental bugler
carried an old cow's-horn, with
which to sound the reveille.

But the bugle which sounded the death-knell of the
great Indian chief Tecumseh was

The Old Wooden Horn of Captain Bob Collins.

It was made of two cedar slabs, three-sixteenths of an
inch in thickness, and these were trimmed and bent so that
when their edges were joined they formed a funnel-shaped
instrument which was about four inches in diameter at the
bell or larger end, and tapered down to a convenient size at
the small end, or mouth-piece.   The two cedar slabs were
held in place by hoops made of cow's-horn.

Whether it was a habit acquired in the army, or whether
Captain Bob was once a flat-boatman, is not recorded, but
certain it is that the doughty Captain always sounded the
reveille at sunrise, and it was not until 1864, when death
called the old man home, that the neighbors, for miles

around, saw the sun rise unheralded by the notes of the quaint instrument.

To make a horn like Captain Bob's requires nice work in steaming, bending, and joining the cedar slabs, but Captain Bob belonged to the Barlow-knife age, and undoubtedly knew how to use one.

Fortunately for boys less skilful than this old pioneer, our ancestors have furnished us another kind of horn, which any boy can make. The original sketches, from which the accompanying diagrams are drawn, were made for the author by a very old gentleman who was himself once a flat-boatman and used the Wabash horn.

This instrument is known as

The Wabash Horn,

(see illustration), for it was among the boatmen from that river that it was always found.

Since the introduction of the house-boat as a popular summer vacation boat, there is no reason why the Wabash horn should not be rescued from the legends of the West and hung under the eaves of every American boy's house-boat, to be used to summon the crew, as it was in the good old times before Fulton filled the waters with his steam-boats and the air with their ear-splitting whistles.

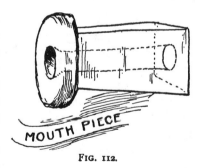

FIG. 112.

The Wabash horn is one of the most primitive affairs possible; it is simply a long box, open at both ends, and differs from an ordinary box in the fact that one end is very much smaller than the opposite end; the big end is the bell of the horn, and the small end is the part you put to your lips.

Among the Flat-boatmen

these horns were made of pine, and sometimes they were as much as eight feet long; but five or six feet will be long enough for any ordinary boy.

Fig. 109 shows a six-foot slab, smoothed and trimmed into proper form. It should be less than a quarter of an inch thick, and made of red-wood, pine, or cedar, which is free from knots, cracks, or blemishes of any kind. Make it four or five inches wide at the big end and two inches wide at the small end, outside measurement. See that the edges are perfectly straight and true; otherwise your horn will leak, and not only be difficult or impossible to blow, but if you do succeed in making a noise with it the notes will be flat and unpleasant. The other three slabs are of the same form as the one described, but to make the openings square two sides must be of dimensions given, and with the other two you must allow for the thickness of the wood, and make them just that much narrower than the first two (Fig. 110).

For a Mouth-piece,

to fit the end of the horn, take a cedar block (Fig. 111) of such dimensions that there will be no risk of splitting it with an auger, and bore a hole through its centre, after which it may be trimmed down to any required dimensions. Next put three sides of your box together and fasten them securely, with small brads.

You can now see the exact form of the small end, and can whittle your cedar mouth-piece (Fig. 112) to fit the little end of the box, and round off the protruding end, as shown in the diagram.

The diagrams of the block and mouth-piece are drawn on a much larger scale than those of the slab and box, that they may be better understood.

With a piece of sand-paper, wrapped around a pine stick, sand-paper the hole in the cedar mouth-piece until it is perfectly smooth. Put the mouth-piece in place, tack on the remaining side to the box, and your Wabash horn is finished.

You can now practise until you learn the bugle-calls, and then hang it under the eaves of your boat, with a just feeling of pride in the knowledge that you are not only a boatman, and a modern wide-awake boy of to-day, but that you lack neither the skill nor the self-reliance of the boy of the day before yesterday.

CHAPTER XIII.

THE AMERICAN BOY'S HOUSE-BOAT.

WHEN the great West of the United States began to attract immigrants from the Eastern coast settlements, the Ohio River rolled between banks literally teeming with all sorts of wild game and wilder men: then it was that the American house-boat had its birth.

The Mississippi, Ohio, and their tributaries furnished

FIG. 113.

highways for easy travel, of which the daring pioneers soon availed themselves.

Lumber was to be had for the labor of felling the trees. From the borders of the Eastern plantations to the prairies, and below the Ohio to the Mississippi, and from the Great Lakes to the Gulf of Mexico, was one vast forest of trees. Trees whose trunks were unscarred by the axe, and whose tall tops reached an altitude which would hardly be believed by those of this generation, who have only seen second, third, or fourth-growth timber.

When the settlement of this new part of the country began it was not long before each stream poured out, with its own flood of water,

A Unique Navy.

There were keel-boats, built something like a modern canal-boat, only of much greater dimensions; there were

146

Bound for a good time

broad-horns, looking like Noah's arks from some
giant's toy-shop, and there were flat-boats and
rafts, the latter with houses built on them, all
recklessly drifting, or being propelled by long
sweeps down the current into the great solemn,
unknown wilderness.

Every island, had it a tongue, could tell of
wrecks; every point or headland, of adventure.

The perils were great and the forest solemn,
but the immigrants were merry, and the squeak-
ing fiddle made the red man rise up from his hiding-place and look with wonder upon the "long
knives" and their squaws dancing on the decks
of their rude crafts, as they swept by into the
unknown.

The advent of the steam-boat gradually drove
the flat-boat, broadhorn, keel-boat, and all the
primitive sweep-propelled craft from the rivers,
but many of the old boatmen were loath to give
up so pleasant a mode of existence, and they built
themselves house-boats, and, still clinging to their
nomadic habits, took their wives, and went to
house-keeping on the bosom of the waters they
loved so well.

Their descendants now form what might well
be called a race of river-dwellers, and to this day
their quaint little arks line the shores of the Mississippi and its tributaries.

Some of These House-Boats

are as crudely made as the Italian huts we see
built along the railroads, but others are neatly
painted, and the interiors are like the prover-

FIG. 114.

bial New England homes, where everything is spick-and-span.

Like the drift-wood, these boats come down the stream with every freshet, and whenever it happens that the waters are particularly high they land at some promising spot and earn a livelihood on the adjacent water, by fishing and working aboard the other river-craft, or they land at some farming district, and as the waters recede they prop up and level their boats, on the bank, with stones or blocks of wood placed under the lower corners of their homes.

The muddy waters, as they retire, leave a long stretch of fertile land between the stranded house and the river, and this space is utilized as a farm, where ducks, chickens, goats and pigs are raised, and where garden-truck grows luxuriantly.

From a boat their home has been transformed to a farm-house; but sooner or later there will be another big freshet, and when the waters reach the late farm-house, lo! it is a boat again, and goes drifting in its happy-go-lucky way down the current. If it escapes the perils of snags and the monster battering-rams, which the rapid current makes of the drifting trees in the flood, it will land again, somewhere, down-stream.

Lately, while on a sketching trip through Kentucky, I was greatly interested in these boats, and on the Ohio River I saw several making good headway against the four-mile-an-hour current. This they did by the aid of

Big Square Sails,

spread on a mast planted near their bows, thus demonstrating the practicability of the use of sails for house-boats.

The house-boats to be described in this article are much

better adapted for sailing than any of the craft used by the water-gypsies of the Western rivers.

For open and exposed waters, like the large lakes which dot many of our inland States, or the Long Island Sound on our coast, the following plans of the American boy's house-boat will have to be altered, but the alterations will be all in the hull. If you make the hull three feet deep it will have the effect of lowering the cabin, while the head-room inside will remain the same. Such a craft can carry a good-

FIG. 115.

sized sail, and weather any gale you are liable to encounter, even on the Sound, during the summer months.

Since the passing away of the glorious old flat-boat days, idle people in England have introduced the

House-Boat as a Fashionable Fad,

which has spread to this country, and the boys now have a new source of fun, as a result of this English fad.

There are still some nooks and corners left in every State in the Union which the greedy pot-hunter and the devouring saw-mill have as yet left undisturbed, and at such places the boy boatmen may "wind their horns," as their ancestors did of old, and have almost as good a time. But first of all they must have a boat, and for convenience the American boy's house-boat will probably be found to excel either a broadhorn or a flat-boat model, it being a link between the two.

The simplest possible house-boat is a Crusoe raft,* with a cabin near the stern and a sand-box for a camp-fire at the bow. A good time can be had aboard even this primitive craft. The next step in evolution is the long open scow, with a cabin formed by stretching canvas over hoops that reach from side to side of the boat (see Fig. 113).

Every boy knows how to build

A Flat-Bottomed Scow,

or at least every boy should know how to make as simple a craft as the scow, but for fear some lad among my readers has neglected this part of his education, I will give a few hints which he may follow.

Building Material.

Select lumber that is free from large knots and other blemishes. Keep the two best boards for the sides of your boat. With your saw cut the side-boards into the form of Fig. 114; see that they are exact duplicates. Set the two pieces parallel to each other upon their straight or top edges, as the first two pieces shown in Fig. 115. Nail on an end-piece at the bow and stern, as the bumper is nailed in Figs. 116 and 117; put the bottom on as shown in Fig. 115, and you have a simple scow.

---

* See p. *100,* "The American Boy's Handy Book."

Centre-Piece.

In Fig. 115 you will notice that there are two sides and a centre-piece, but this centre-piece is not necessary for the ordinary open boat, shown by Fig. 113. Here you have one of the simple forms of house-boat, and you can make it of dimensions to suit your convenience. I will not occupy space with the details of this boat, because they may be seen by a glance at the diagrams, and my purpose is to tell you how to build the American boy's house-boat, which is a more elegant craft than the rude open scow, with a can-vas-covered cabin, shown by Fig. 113.

The Sides of the House-Boat

are 16 feet long, and to make them you need some sound two-inch planks. After selecting the lumber plane it off and make the edges true and straight. Each side and the centre-piece should now measure exactly 16 feet in length by 14 inches in width, and about 2 inches thick. Cut off from each end of each piece a triangle, as shown by the dotted lines at G, H, I (Fig. 114); from H to G is 1 foot, and from H to I is 7 inches. Measure from H to I, 7 inches, and mark the point. Then measure from H to G, 12 inches, and mark the point. Then, with a carpenter's pencil, draw a line from G to I, and saw along this line. Keep the two best planks for the sides of your boat, and use the one that is left for the centre-piece. Measure 2 feet on the top or straight edge of your centre-piece, and mark the point, A (Fig. 114). From A measure 8 feet 10 inches, and mark the point C (Fig. 114).

With a carpenter's square rule the lines A, B and C, D, and make them each 10 inches long, then rule the line, B,

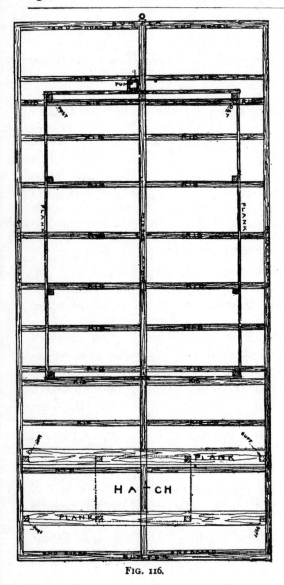

FIG. 116.

D (Fig. 114). The piece A, B, C, D must now be carefully cut out; this can be done by using the saw to cut A, B and D, C. Then, about 6 inches from A, saw another line of the same length, and with a chisel cut the block out. You then have room to insert a rip-saw, at B, and can saw along the line B, D until you reach D, when the piece may be removed, leaving the space A, B, D, C for the cabin of the boat (see Figs. 116 and 117).

At a point 9 inches from the bow of the boat make a mark on the centre-piece, and another mark 5 inches farther

away, at F (Fig. 114). With the saw cut a slit at each mark,
1 inch deep, and with a chisel cut out, as shown by the dotted
lines ; do the same at E, leaving a space of 1½ feet between
the two notches, which are made to allow the two planks
shown in the plan (Fig. 116), to rest on. These planks support the deck and the hatch, at the locker in the bow. The
notches at E and F are not on the side-boards, the planks
being supported at the sides by uprights, Figs. 116 and 117.

All that now remains to be done with the centre-piece is
to saw some three-cornered notches on bottom edge, one at
bow, one at stern, and one or two amidships; this is to allow
the water which may leak in to flow freely over the whole
bottom, and to prevent it from gathering at one side and
causing your craft to rest upon an uneven keel.

Next select a level piece of ground near by and arrange
the three pieces upon some supports, as shown in Fig. 115,
so that from outside to outside of side-pieces it will measure just 8 feet across the bow and stern. Of 1-inch board

Make Four End-Pieces,

for the bow and stern (see A, A', Fig. 115), to fit between
the sides and centre-piece. Make them each a trifle wider
than H, I, Fig. 114, so that after they have been fitted they
can be trimmed down with a plane, and bevelled on the same
slant as the bottom at G, I, Fig. 114. It being 8 feet between the outside of each centre-piece, and the sides and the
centre-piece being each 2 inches thick, that gives us 8 feet
— 6 inches, or 7½ feet as the combined length of A and A'
(Fig. 115). In other words, each end-piece will be half of
7½ feet long—that is, 3 feet 9 inches long. After making
the four end-pieces, each 3 feet 9, by 9 inches, fit the ends in
place so that there is an inch protruding above and below.
See that your bow and stern are perfectly square, and nail

with wire nails through the sides into A and A′; toe-nail at the centre-piece—that is, drive the nails from the broad side of A and A′ slantingly, into the centre-piece, after which trim down with your plane the projecting inch on bottom, to agree with the slant of the bottom of the boat.

Now for the Bottom.

This is simple work. All that is necessary is to have straight, true edges to your one-inch planks, fit them to-

FIG. 117.—Cross-Section of Boat.

gether, and nail them in place. Of course, when you come to the slant at bow and stern the bottom-boards at each end will have to have a bevelled edge, to fit snugly against the boards on the flat part of the bottom of the boat; but any boy who is accustomed to shake the gray matter in his brain can do this. Remember, scientists say that thought is the agitation of the gray matter of the brain, and if you are going to build a boat or play a good game of football you must shake up that gray stuff, or the other boys will put you down as a "stuff." No boy can expect to be successful in building a boat, of even the crudest type, unless he keeps his wits about him, so I shall take it for granted that there are no " stuffs" among my readers.

After the boards are all snugly nailed on the bottom, and fitted together so that there are no cracks to calk up, the hull is ready to have

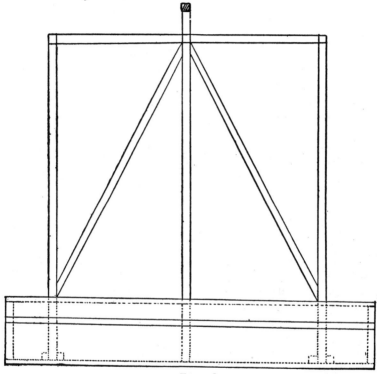

FIG. 118.

The Bumpers

nailed in place, at bow and stern. See the plan, Fig. 116, and the elevation, Fig. 117. The bumpers must be made of 2-inch plank, 8 feet long by about 9 inches wide; wide

enough to cover A and A′ of Fig. 115, and to leave room
for a bevel at the bottom edge to meet the slant of the
bow and stern, and still have room at the top to cover the
edge of the deck to the hull (see Fig. 117).

The Hull May Now be Painted,

with two coats of good paint, and after it is dry may be
turned over and allowed to rest on a number of round
sticks, called rollers.

If you will examine Fig. 116 you will see there

Twenty-odd Ribs.

These are what are called two-by-fours—that is, 2 inches
thick by 4 inches wide. They support the floor of the
cabin and forward locker, at the same time adding strength
to the hull.

The ribs are each the same length as the end-board, A and
A′ of Fig. 115, and are nailed in place in the same manner.
Each bottom-rib must have a notch 2 inches deep cut in
the bottom edge to allow the free passage of water, so as to
enable you to pump dry. Commencing at the stern, the
distance between the inside of the bumper and the first
rib is 1 foot 6 inches. This is a deck-rib, as may be seen by
reference to Figs. 116 and 117. After measuring 1½ feet
from the bumper, on inside of side-board, mark the point
with a carpenter's pencil. Measure the same distance on
the centre-piece, and mark the point as before; then carefully fit your rib in flush or even with the top of the side-
piece, and fasten it in place by nails driven through the side-
board into the end of the rib, and toe-nailed to centre-piece.
Do the same with its mate on the other side of centre-
piece.

The Cabin of this House-Boat

is to fit in the space, A, B, D, C of the centre-piece, Fig. 114. There is to be a 1-inch plank at each end (see Fig. 117), next to which the side-supports at each end of cabin fit. The supports are two-by-twos; so, allowing 1 inch for the plank and 2 inches for the upright support, the next pair of ribs will be just 3 inches from A B, Fig. 114, of the centre-piece (see Figs. 116 and 117). The twin ribs at the forward end of the cabin will be the same distance from D C, Fig. 114, as shown in the plan and elevation, Figs. 116 and 117. This leaves five pairs of ribs to be distributed between the front and back end of the cabin. From the outside of each end-support to the inside of the nearest middle-support is 2 feet 6 inches. Allowing 2 inches for the supports, this will place the adjoining ribs 2 feet 8 inches from the outside of the end-supports. The other ribs are placed midway between, as may be seen by the elevation, Fig. 117.

There is another pair of

Deck-Ribs

at the forward end of the cabin, which are placed flush with the line D, C, Fig. 114 (see Figs. 116 and 117). The two pairs of ribs in the bow are spaced, as shown in the diagram. This description may appear as if it was a complicated affair; but you will find it a simple thing to work out if you will remember to allow space for your pump in the stern, space for the end-planks at after and forward end of cabin, and space for your uprights. The planks at after and forward end of cabin are to box in the cabin floor.

The Boat May Now be Launched

by sliding it over the rollers, which will not be found a difficult operation.

The Plans Show Three Lockers

—two in the bow under the hatch and one under the rear bunk—but if it is deemed necessary the space between-decks, at each side of the cabin, may be utilized as lockers. In this space you can store enough truck to last for months. A couple of doors in the plank at the front of the cabin opening, under the deck, will be found very convenient to reach the forward locker in wet weather.

FIG. 119.

The Keel

is a triangular piece of 2-inch board, made to fit exactly in the middle of the stern, and had best be nailed in place before the boat is launched (see Fig. 117). The keel must have its bottom edge flush with the bottom of the boat, and a strip of hard-wood nailed on the stern-end of the keel and bumper, as shown in the diagram. A couple of strong screw-eyes will support the rudder.

After the boat is launched the

Side-Supports for the Cabin May be Erected.

These are "two-by-twos" and eight in number, and each 5 feet 9 inches long. Nail them securely at their lower ends to the adjoining ribs. See that they are plumb, and fasten them temporarily with diagonal pieces, to hold the top ends in place, while you nail down the lower deck or flooring.

Now fit and nail the two 1-inch planks in place, at the bow and stern-end of the cabin, each of which has its top one inch above the sides, even with the proposed deck (see dotted lines in Fig. 117).

Use Ordinary Flooring,

or if that is not obtainable use ¾-inch pine boards, and run them lengthwise from the bow to the front end of the cabin and along the sides of the cabin. Then floor the cabin lengthwise from bow to stern. This gives you a dry cabin floor, for there are 4 inches of space underneath for bilge water, which unless your boat is badly made and very leaky, is plenty of room for what little water may leak in from above or below. The two side-boards of the cabin floor must, of course, have square places neatly cut out to fit the uprights of the cabin. This may be done by slipping the floor-board up against the uprights and carefully marking the places with a pencil where they will come through the board, and then at each mark sawing two inches in the floor plank, and cutting out the blocks with a chisel.

The Hatch.

Now take a " four-by-four " and saw off eight short supports for the two 1-inch planks which support the hatch, Figs. 116 and 117. Toe-nail the middle four-by-four to the floor in such a position that the two cross-planks (which are made to fit in the notches E and F, Fig. 114) will rest on the supports. Nail the four other supports to the sideboards of your boat, and on top of these nail the cross-planks, as shown in the diagrams.

The boat is now ready for its

Upper Deck

of 1-inch pine boards. These are to be nailed on lengthwise, bow and stern and at sides of cabin, leaving, of course, the cabin open, as shown by the position of the boys in Fig. 117, and an opening, 3 feet by 2, for the hatch (Fig. 116). The two floors will act as benches for the uprights of the cabin, and hold them stiff and plumb.

To further stiffen the frame, make two diagonals for the stern-end, as shown in Fig. 118, and nail them in place.

The Rafters,

or roof-rods, should extend a foot each way beyond the cabin, hence cut them two feet longer than the cabin, and after testing your uprights, to see that they are exactly

piumb, nail the two side roof-rods in place (see dotted lines
in Fig. 117). The cross-pieces at the ends, as they support
no great weight, may be fitted be-
tween the two side-rods, and nailed
there.

The roof is to be made of ½-
inch boards bent into a curve, and
the ridge-pole, or centre roof-rod,
must needs have some support.
This is obtained by two short pieces
of 2-by-4, each 6 inches long, which
are toe-nailed to the centre of each
cross-rod, and the ridge-pole nailed
to their tops. At 3 feet from the
upper deck the side frame-pieces
are toe-nailed to the uprights. As
may be seen, there are three two-
by-fours on each side (Fig. 117).

The space between the side
frame-pieces, the two middle up-
rights, and side roof-rods, is where the windows are to be
placed.

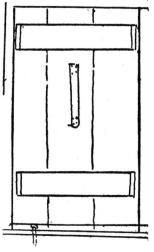

FIG. 120.—Inside View of Door.

Use ½-inch (tongue and groove preferred) pine boards
for sidings, and

Box in your Cabin

neatly, allowing space for windows on each side, as indicated. Leave the front open. Of the same kind of boards
make your roof; the boards being light you can bend them
down upon each side and nail them to the side roof-rods,
forming a pretty curve, as may be seen in the illustration
of the American boy's house-boat.

This Roof,

to be finished neatly and made entirely water-proof, should be covered with tent-cloth or light canvas, smoothly stretched over and tacked upon the under side of the pro-jecting edges. Three good coats of paint will make it water-proof and pleasant to look upon.

The description, so far, has been for a neatly finished craft, but I have seen very serviceable and comfortable house-boats built of rough lumber, in which case the curved roof, when they had one, had nar-row strips nailed over the boards where they joined each other.

To Contrive a Movable Front

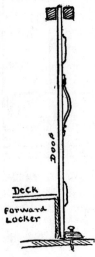

FIG. 121.—Side-View of Door.

to your cabin, make two doors to fit and close the front opening, but in place of hanging the doors on hinges, set them in place. Each door should have a good strong strap nailed securely on the inside, for a handle, and a batten or cross-piece at top and bottom of inside surface. A two-by-four, run parallel to the front top cross-frame and nailed there, just a sufficient distance from it to allow the top of the door to be inserted between, will hold the top of the door securely. A two-by-four, with bolt-holes near either end to correspond with bolt-holes in the floor, will hold the bottom when the door is pushed in place, the movable bottom-piece shoved against it and the bolts thrust in (see Fig. 120, view from inside of cabin. Fig. 121, side-view). It will be far less work to break in the side of the

cabin than to burst in such doors, if they are well made.
These doors possess this advantage: they can be removed
and used as table-tops, leaving the whole front open to the
summer breeze, or one may be removed, and still allow
plenty of ventilation. A moulding on deck around the
cabin is not necessary, but it will add finish and prevent
the rain-water from leaking in.

To lock up the boat you must set the doors from the
inside, and if you wish to leave the craft locked you must
crawl out of the window and fasten the latter with a padlock.

Fig. 122 shows the construction of

The Rudder,

and also an arrangement by which it may be worked from
the front of the boat, which, when the boat is towed, will
be found most convenient.

The hatch should be made of 1-inch boards, to fit snugly
flush with the deck, as in the illustration, or made of 2-inch
plank, and a moulding fitted around the opening, as shown
in Fig. 117.

A Pair of Rowlocks,

made of two round oak sticks with an iron rod in their
upper ends, may be placed in holes in the deck near the
bow, and the boat can be propelled by two oarsmen using
long "sweeps," which have holes at the proper places to
fit over the iron rods projecting from the oaken rowlocks.
These rowlocks may be removed when not in use, and the
holes closed by wooden plugs, while the sweeps can be
hung at the side of the cabin, under its eaves, or lashed
fast to the roof.

Two or more Ash Poles,

for pushing or poling the boat over shallow water or other difficult places for navigation are handy, and should not be left out of the equipment.   The window-sashes may be hung on hinges and supplied with hooks and screw-eyes to fasten them open by hooking them to the eaves when it is desired to let in the fresh air, as shown in the illustration of the finished boat.

Two bunks can be fitted at the rear end of the cabin, one above the other, the bottom bunk being the lid to a locker (see Fig. 117).

The Locker

is simply a box, the top of which is just below the deck-line and extending the full width of the cabin.   It has hinges at the back, and may be opened for the storage of luggage.

Over the lid blankets are folded, making a divan during the day and a bed at night.

The top bunk is made like the frame of a cheap cot, but in place of being upholstered it has a strong piece of canvas stretched across it.   This bunk is also hinged to the back of the cabin, so that when not in use it can be swung up against the roof and fastened there as the top berth in a sleeping-car is fastened.   Four 4-by-4 posts can be bolted to the side-support at each corner of the bottom bunk; they will amply support the top bunk, as the legs do a table-top when the frame is allowed to rest upon their upper ends.   This makes accommodation for two boys, and there is still room for upper and lower side bunks, the cabin being but six feet wide.   If you put bunks on both sides you will be rather crowded, it is true, but by allow-

ing a 1-foot passage in the middle, you can have two side
bunks and plenty of head room. This will accommodate
four boys, and that is a full crew for a boat of this size.

On board a yacht I have often seen four full-grown men
crowded into a smaller space in the cabin, while the sailor-
men in the fo'castle had not near that amount of breathing-
room.

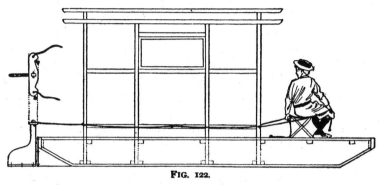

Fig. 122.

Figs. 118, 119, and 120 show

A More Simple Set of Plans.

Here the cabin is built on top of the upper deck, and
there are no bottom-ribs, the uprights being held in place
by blocks nailed to the bottom of the boat, and by the deck
of the boat. This is secure enough for well-protected
waters, small lakes, and small streams. Upon the inland
streams of New York State I have seen two-story house-
boats, the cabin, or house, being only a frame-work covered
with canvas. One such craft I saw in central New York,
drifting down-stream over a shallow riff, and as it bumped
along over the stones it presented a strange sight. The
night was intensely dark, and the boat brightly lighted.
The lights shone through the canvas covering, and this big

luminous house went bobbing over the shallow water, while shouts of laughter and the "plinky-plunk" of a banjo told in an unmistakable manner of the jolly time the crew were having.

Canvas-Cabined House-Boat.

If you take an ordinary open scow and erect a frame of uprights and cross-pieces, and cover it with canvas, you will have just such a boat as the one seen in central New York. This boat may be propelled by oars, the rowers sitting under cover, and the canvas being lifted at the sides to allow the sweeps to work; but of course it will not be as snug as the well-made American boy's house-boat, neither can it stand the same amount of rough usage, wind, and rain as the latter boat.

In the illustration the reader will notice a stove-pipe at the stern; there is room for a small stove back of the cabin, and in fair weather it is much better to cook outside than inside the cabin. When you tie up to the shore for any length of time, a rude shelter of boughs and bark will make a good kitchen on the land, in which the stove may be placed, and you will enjoy all the fun of a camp, with the advantage of a snug house to sleep in.

For the benefit of boys who doubt their ability to build a boat of this description, it may be well to state that other lads have used these directions and plans with successful results, and their boats now gracefully float on many waters, a source of satisfaction and pride to their owners.

Information for Old Boys.

On all the Western rivers small flat-boats or scows are to be had at prices which vary in accordance with the mercantile instincts of the purchaser, and with the desire of the seller to dispose of his craft. Such boats are propelled by "sweeps," a name used to designate the long poles with boards on their outer edges that serve as blades and form the oars. These boats are often supplied with a deck-house, extending almost from end to end, and if such a house is lacking one may be built with little expense. The cabin may be divided into rooms and the sleeping apartments supplied with cheaply made bunks. It is not the material of the bunk which makes it comfortable—it is the mattress in the bunk upon which your comfort will depend. The kitchen and dining-room may be all in one. An awning spread over the roof will make a delightful place in which to lounge and catch the river breezes.

The Cost of House-Boats.

The cost of a ready-made flat-bottomed house-boat is anywhere from thirty dollars to one or more thousands. In Florida such a boat, 40 by 20 feet, built for the quiet waters of the St. John's River or its tributaries, or the placid lagoons, will cost eight hundred dollars. This boat is well painted outside and rubbed down to a fine oil finish inside; it has one deck, and the hull is used for toilet apartments and state-rooms; the hull is well calked and all is in good trim. Such expense is, however, altogether unnecessary—there need be no paint or polish. All you need is a well-calked hull and a water-tight roof of boards or canvas overhead; cots or bunks to sleep in; chairs, stools, boxes or benches to sit on; hammocks to loll in, and a good supply of provisions in the larder.

House-boats for the open waters are necessarily more expensive. As a rule they need round bottoms that stand well out of the water, and are built like the hull of a ship. These boats cost as much to build as a small yacht. From twelve to fifteen hundred dollars will build a good house-boat, with comfortable sleeping-berths, toilet-rooms, and store-rooms below; a kitchen, dining-room and living-room on the cabin deck, with wide, breezy passageways separating them.

If a bargain can be found in an old schooner with a good hull, for two or three hundred dollars, a first-class house-boat can be made by the expenditure of as much more for a cabin. The roofs of all house-boats should extend a foot or more beyond the sides of the cabin.

For People of Limited Means.

For people with little money to spend, these expensive boats are as much out of reach as a yacht, but they may often be rented for prices within the means of people in moderate circumstances. At New York I have known a good schooner-yacht, 84 feet over all, to be chartered for two weeks, with crew of skipper and two men, the larder plentifully supplied with provisions and luxuries for six people and the crew, making nine in all, at a cost of thirty-six dollars apiece for each of the six passengers. An equally good house-boat should not cost over twelve dollars a week per passenger for a party of ten. In inland waters, if a boat could be rented, the cost should not exceed seven or eight dollars a week per passenger.

A canal-boat is a most excellent house-boat for a pleasure party, either on inland streams or along our coast.

Street-Car Cabins.

Since the introduction of cable and trolley cars the street-car companies have been selling their old horse-cars, in some instances at figures below the cost of the window-glass in them; so cheap, in fact, that poor people buy them to use as woodsheds and chicken-coops.

One of these cars will make an ideal cabin for a house-boat, and can be adapted for that purpose with little or no alterations. All it needs is a good flat-boat to rest in, and you have a palatial house-boat.

CHAPTER XIV.

A BACK-YARD SWITCHBACK.

THE back-yard affords an opportunity to build a summer toboggan slide, or its equivalent, commonly known as a

"Switchback,"

the difference being that, in place of toboggans, cars are used, and in place of ice and snow you coast down a railroad track.

The Wheels

of the back-yard "switchback" car must be made of thick, sound wood, and if there is a wood-working factory in your neighborhood it will save you time and trouble to go there and have the wheels sawed out with the machinery which they have built for that kind of work. But if you must do it yourself, then select a piece of two-inch plank, and after driving a tack in the centre, fasten a string to the tack and attach a soft pencil to the opposite end of the string. With this describe a circle about nine inches in diameter, or measuring about four and a half inches from the tack to the pencil.

With a hand-saw roughly cut out the wheel, using great care to only touch the circle with the saw, but in no case to cut through the circumference. You will now have an irregular wheel, with a number of flat surfaces for its edge (Fig. 123 A).

In this way you may continue to saw off the triangular corners until you reduce the wheel to a condition where it only needs the application of a sharp knife to round the edge until it corresponds with the pencil circle.

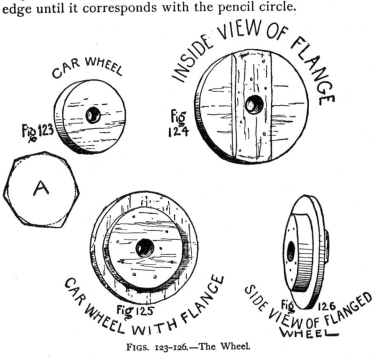

FIGS. 123–126.—The Wheel.

What is called

The Flange

of the wheel is practically another wheel, made of thinner material (Fig. 124), which is securely nailed to the first wheel (Figs. 125 and 126), with the grain of the wood of the flange crossing the grain of the wood of the wheel proper at right angles. The flange is made of one-inch

board, and to prevent its splitting is reënforced by a strip
of wood fastened on across the grain, with screws, as shown
in Fig. 124.

When the four wheels are finished, and a hole large
enough for a good strong axle is bored in the exact centre
of each, you will be ready to begin work upon the car.

Set the Car-Bed Low.

The smallest boy will understand that the lower the bed
of the car is put the less the danger of an upset, so instead
of putting the axle, under
the car, run them through
the bed, as shown by Fig.
128.

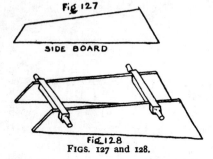

FIGS. 127 and 128.

Build the Axles

of four-by-four timber, and
by the aid of a drawing-
knife or a good, strong,
sharp jack-knife, trim off
the ends of the timber to
the form shown in the diagram.

When the ends are small enough to allow the wheels
to revolve freely, saw out places in the side-boards of the
car (Figs. 127 and 128), into which the square part of the
axle will snugly fit.

The Bottom of the Car

may be made of half-inch boards, which can be joined and
nailed on to the car, with their irregular ends protruding,
after which, with a hand-saw, cut off the ends even with the
side-boards, as in Fig. 129.

Then nail in place the head and tail-boards, and in the same manner saw off their protruding ends, even with the side-boards (Fig. 129). To finish your car it is only necessary to slip the wheels upon the axles. The wheels may be held in place by pegs of hard-wood driven through holes in the hub, made for that purpose, as shown in Fig. 130. You will then have a car, but no track to run it upon. However, if you build the toboggan slide which is described in the next chapter, you may lay rails, made of two-

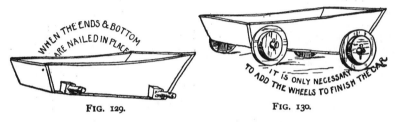

FIG. 129.   FIG. 130.

by-four timber, down your toboggan slide and thus transform it into a back-yard "switchback."

But if you have no toboggan slide you will have to build a tramway for your car against the back fence, wood-shed, or any other suitable place.

In the diagram (Fig. 135) here given, the slide is shown as it would be if built against the back fence, extending forward through the middle of the yard. But you must have a

Starting Platform.

You will need four pieces of timber, seven feet long and two inches thick by four inches wide, for the uprights or corner-posts (A and B, Fig. 131), unless the posts and rails of the back fence are on your side of the yard, as in Fig. 132. In this case you need only two seven-foot sticks and two short ones, to fit on the top rail of the fence. The tops of

these short posts should be just seven feet from the ground.
Nail them securely in place, about five feet apart, as in Fig.
132, and then see that the fence-boards, to which the posts

IF THIS SIDE
OF THE FENCE
FACES YOUR
YARD

NAIL TWO
UPRIGHTS (A & B)
AGAINST THE FENCE

FIG. 131.

are nailed, are secure.   If they are not secure, climb over
the fence and put in a few good wire nails, for if the fence
is not strong your structure will be weak.   Additional
strength may be gained by making each of the uprights of

two pieces of two-by-four, nailed together, thus making the posts four-by-four.

BUT
IF IT IS THIS SIDE,
NAIL TWO SHORT
UPRIGHTS
on top of the
FENCE RAIL

FIG. 132.

It is a good plan to erect one of the posts directly over one of the fence-posts; this will add strength and stiffness to the structure. If you have any doubts about the ability of the fence to support the platform, erect two seven-foot posts, as in Fig. 131, and spike them to the top and bottom rail of the fence. Next take two pieces of two-by-four and notch them, as E and F are notched in Fig. 133. Nail F to

FIG. 133.

the top of A and B, and E to the ends of C and D, the two seven-foot posts of two-by-four. Near the other ends of these last posts nail a cross-piece (G, Fig. 133), and then, to stiffen the frame, turn it over and nail on two diagonal pieces of lighter material.

Erect this frame about five or six feet from the fence and secure it in place by the two diagonals, H and H (Fig. 133),

FIG. 134.

which are nailed near the top of C and D, and "toe-nailed" to the bottom rail of the fence.

From the bottom rail of the fence, and level with it, run
the two J pieces of board to C and D, and nail them securely, as in Fig. 134; then nail on the two top side-pieces, K
and K, and the framework of the starting platform is ready
for its floor.   Nail boards across the top, from E to F, and
saw off the protruding ends, as in Fig. 134.

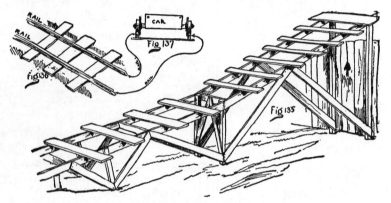

FIGS. 135, 136, and 137.

The Track

must be a "straight-away," which means no curves to round,
hence you must build it in the position which will give
the longest run for your trouble.

A Curved Track

means more difficult work on the tramway and cars, for the
car must have a movable axle in order to be able to round
the curve.   But with a straight track the play of the wheel
upon the hub should allow enough freedom of motion to
overcome the little inaccuracy which may occur in the rails.
Experiment will teach you just what is needed.   I cannot

give exact rules, because the material and location will differ with each builder, and I have found that when I give positive rules, the rules are followed, even when the material and location are entirely unsuited to the directions given. For this reason it is best for each boy to experiment for himself.

Erect the Uprights

first, and brace them with the diagonal boards, as shown in the diagram (Fig. 135). When you are certain the structure is firm and can stand the strain and weight of a loaded car, lay the two-by-four rails upon the ground, and fit them to the car-wheels by pushing the car over them, to see that they are just the right distance apart. If you make your track too wide the car-wheels will slip off the rails and run between them, and if you lay your track with too narrow a gauge the rails will pinch the flanges of the wheels so tightly that the car will stop, or the rails spread.

When one section of the track is laid and it is found that the car runs freely upon it, nail cross-ties of ordinary boards across from rail to rail, like a ladder. Then take the ladder, and turning it over so that the rails are on top (Fig. 136), adjust it to the tramway (Fig. 135), and fasten it securely, by nailing the cross-ties to the side-boards of the tramway.

In Fig. 135

The Cross-ties, or Sleepers,

are put in position, to show how they will look when the track is laid, but in reality the cross-ties must be nailed to the rails while the latter are upon the level ground, as I have already stated.

When each section of track is fastened in place, from the top of the tramway to the ground, and as much farther as your space or lumber will admit, load your car with stones, or some equally heavy freight, and start it down the "switchback."

If the car reaches its journey's end with no mishap, you can with safety get in the car for the next trip and coast down yourself and a jolly good coast it will be.

The plans (Figs. 135 and 136) may be altered so that the car will run down one hill and mount another not quite so high, and many other improvements will suggest themselves to the young civil engineers who build this "switchback," but the first track you erect should be as simple as is consistent with strength and safety, and the improvements left to some future time.

Ticket-Chopper's Box.

You may then take a square box, with a lock and key attached, and bore a hole in one end large enough to admit a good-sized marble; use this as the railroad and ferry-men use a ticket-chopper's box, let every boy who wants a ride drop a marble in the box.

Some thirty years ago a certain boy built a "switchback" in his back-yard, very much like the one here described, and great fun he had with it; but as he was not rich, and the lumber cost him something, he issued a number of tickets at one cent each, every ticket entitling the holder to three rides on the "switchback." In this way he was soon repaid all the expense he had been under during the erection of his wonderful railroad.

This is what that boy told the writer, and as the former young engineer is now no longer a lad, but a grave D.D.,

Under Full Headway.

who wears solemn black clothes and preaches long sermons, the writer believes him.

But whether you charge a cent, a marble, or nothing, for a ride, you and your friends are bound to have a rollicking good time on the back-yard "switchback."

CHAPTER XV.

HOW TO BUILD A TOBOGGAN-SLIDE IN THE BACK-YARD.

TOBOGGANS and sleds are not always used on snow and ice, neither is coasting confined to winter weather.

At most of the summer resorts you may coast down an artificial hill, upon real toboggans, over a slide of hard-wood rollers, and end with a whoop and a splash in the water of the bathing-pool.

Slipperies.

All through the southwestern part of this country the summer drought causes the rivers to subside, leaving more or less high mud or clay banks, which are utilized by the youngsters as mud-slides, and called by them "slipperies." The boys use neither sled nor toboggan, but make a slide by pouring water over the dry mud until they have a long, slippery track, down which they coast, ending with a splash in the river.

A War-Time Slippery.

A good many years ago a battalion of Union soldiers were camped on the river-bank, near where some Kentucky boys were having fun on a long slippery, and one day, before the lads knew what had happened, two thousand naked men suddenly made their appearance, jostling each other, for a slide down the mud-track. It was a great sight to

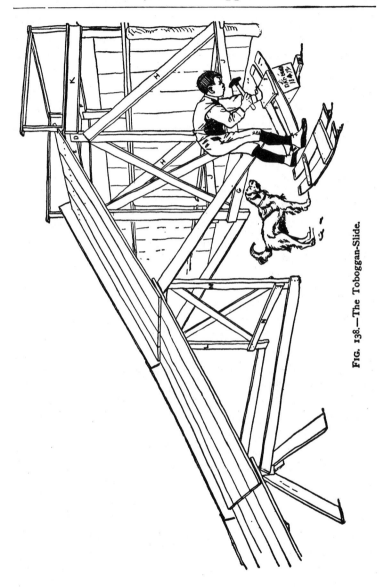

FIG. 138.—The Toboggan-Slide.

see these men-children coasting down the mud-bank, and the show the soldiers made for them repaid the boys for their labor in building the slide.

Tropical Toboggan-Slide.

Under the torrid zone, away out on the Islands of the Pacific Ocean, the natives coast down-hill, in the hottest weather, on the dry grass, and where that does not exist they build themselves toboggan-slides, with slabs of smooth lava. Hundreds of these tracks line the mountainsides near the native villages. The sled these daring coasters use is from seven to twenty feet long, and as narrow in proportion as a shell-boat, there being only a few inches of space between the very hard, polished wooden runners. It takes both skill and pluck to ride one of these cranky tropical sleds, or toboggans, but the natives possess both of these qualities, and without a thought of failure pick up their primitive machine, take a short, swift run, and throw the sled and themselves together, headlong down the lava-slide. There follows a wildly exciting and breathless ride down the incline, and a scoot over the level country, until gradually the queer sled slows up and comes to a stop; and then there is a long climb back, for another daring coast to the quiet valley below.

In the United States we have no smooth lava with which to build slides on our native hills, and if we did have the lava-slides only a few of our boys would have an opportunity to use them.

When the snow covers the ground it is not every boy who can find a convenient hill where he may enjoy the healthful fun of coasting. A great many boys live in a level country, and hundreds and thousands of others have their homes in cities and towns, where heavy carts, policemen, and trolley-cars, make coasting a forbidden pleasure. However, with a real toboggan-slide in the back-yard, a boy may snap his fingers at a level country, lumbering carts, death-dealing cars, and meddlesome guardians of the peace.

In a day's time three boys can build a slide; but, of course, it cannot be built without some labor. If it could, it would be of no value. The labor consists only in sawing a few pieces of timber and driving a few nails to hold the frame together, and it is effort well-spent.

If Your Back-Yard is Wide

enough you can run the toboggan-track alongside the back fence, with the starting platform built in the fence-corner, backing against the side fence. In this way your slide will occupy but little space.

But if Your Yard is Long and Narrow,

build your platform against the back fence (as described in Chapter XIV.), and let the track run along one of the side fences.

The most difficult part of the work is now finished. Make

A Frame,

on the pattern of C, E, D, G (Figs. 133 and 134, Chapter XIV.), and about half the height of the platform (see L, M, N, Fig. 138).

Erect this frame in front of the platform, and at such a distance from it as will allow your longest boards to span the intervening space, as in Fig. 138. Nail two diagonals —one at each top end of the frame M, L, N, and fasten the opposite ends of the diagonals to the bottoms of C and D.

Long boards may be laid from the ground to the top of M, N, L, and nailed securely to the frame, and other boards laid over the upper ends of the first, and the top of E, where they can be securely nailed, and the slide is ready for use.

The Incline May be Lengthened

by using a carpenter's wooden horse for another frame, and allowing the boards from the ground to rest on this, and another set of boards run from this to L, M, N, as in Fig. 138, or as described for the switchback, in the preceding chapter.

With plenty of snow on the ground it will not hurt a strong boy to fall from this track.   But there may not be much snow on the hard, frozen ground, or your little brothers and sisters may be fond of coasting.   To prevent any mishap, a guard-rail, such as is shown on one side of the slide in Fig. 138, should be nailed on each side of the inclined plane, as shown in the diagram.

The posts for the railing around the platform are "toe-nailed" to the floor, and the rail is nailed on top of them. In case the rail seems weak, a diagonal or two, like those on the slide-frames, will make it sufficiently strong.

A Toboggan Room.

By boarding up around the posts, under the platform, a small room will be made, at a trifling additional cost and labor, which can be kept warm, and will afford a means of shelter and a place to lock up the sleds.

An excellent plan for

"Packing" the Slide, or Chute,

is to mix sawdust and snow together, in equal parts, using just enough water to cause it to pack solidly, as a foundation for the top crust of snow or ice. This foundation will make the top ice or snow last much longer, in thawing weather, than it would if spread directly on the wooden bed of the slide. If the snow in the chute is properly and smoothly banked up on this composition foundation, moistened and frozen hard, with the addition of half an inch of fresh snow on top, the slide, in ordinary weather, will last all winter.

It is a Wise Plan

to be ready for any emergency. You may have visitors who come without sleds, and who would have but a chilly time watching the others coast down the wonderful toboggan-slide. To prevent the chance of any such disagreeable occurrences, knock an old barrel to pieces and build yourself a supply of toboggans with the staves. Two barrel-staves, fastened together by a cross-bar in front and a piece of board for a seat in the rear, will make a most excellent toboggan.

The boy in the foreground of Fig. 138 is building toboggans of barrel staves, and a glance at this cut will tell you how they are made.

PART II

RAINY DAY IDEAS

CHAPTER XVI.

A HOME-MADE CIRCUS.

To the typical American boy every object he sees suggests to him possibilities of amusement, and to him an up-to-date bath-room is as full of such suggestions as a dictionary is of words. The great white tub affords an excellent sea for his gun-boats to do battle upon, or offers a straight-away course over which his home-made yachts may sail, while a fan fills their sails with everything from a light breeze to a ripping gale.

What boy has not discovered, for himself, that

The Bath-tub is a Splendid Receiving-Tank

for the occasional water-animals captured by him in creek or pond, or at the fish-market?

The laundry tubs are also useful and, not being in demand as frequently as the bath-tub, are for this reason often more convenient.

If the grown people would only let the bath-room alone, there is no end to the fun which an ingenious lad could have in that useful little room.

As a Lake for His Fleet,

and as a receiving-tank for his water-pets are only two of the uses which the bath-tub suggests to a bright boy. When he sees the faucet he realizes that this can afford him power for all sorts of machinery, if he can arrange a water-wheel under it to transmit the power.

Every country boy knows how to make water-wheels, and every summer the springs and brooks all over the land turn these little wheels in exactly the same manner which the larger streams turn the big wheels for the factories and mills on their banks.

But there are thousands of boys in our great cities who have never seen

A Water-wheel,

and for the use of these boys the accompanying illustrations were drawn.

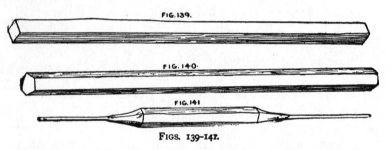

FIG. 139.

FIG. 140.

FIG. 141

FIGS. 139-141.

Fig. 139 shows a four-sided soft-pine stick, with square ends, and if you have a good sharp knife it requires but little work to trim off the four edges of this stick until it has the form of a six-sided lead-pencil (Fig. 140), after which but little skill is required to whittle the ends down to the size of the hole in a thread-spool (Fig. 141).

The Shaft.

You will see, on examining the illustration, that the middle is left with the six sides untouched.

An Old Cigar-Box

will not only furnish you with excellent wood for the paddles of your wheels (Fig. 142), but, if carefully taken apart, it will also furnish you with just the right sort of nails with which to fasten your paddles to the shaft.

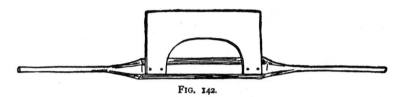

FIG. 142.

Make Six Paddles,

all of the same size and same pattern, and nail one to one of the six sides of the shaft (Fig. 142).

Turn the shaft around to the next face or side, and nail

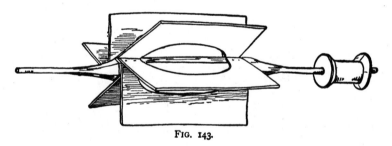

FIG. 143.

another paddle in place; continue this work until you have the paddle-wheel shown in Fig. 143.

On to one or both ends of the shaft you may now slip wooden spools, pushing them up the stick until they fit tightly, and leave a projecting end of the shaft sticking out of the end of the spool.

Hanging-Bars.

Next take a lath or stick of some kind, which is of such
length that it will rest securely when laid across from side
to side of the bath-tub. To this stick tack two others, as
shown in Fig. 144.

These hanging-bars must be long enough to allow
the water-wheel to be suspended just below the faucet of
the bath-tub. Strengthen your hanging-bars (Fig. 144) by
two diagonal pieces.

Fig. 145 shows how to cut a notch near the lower end of

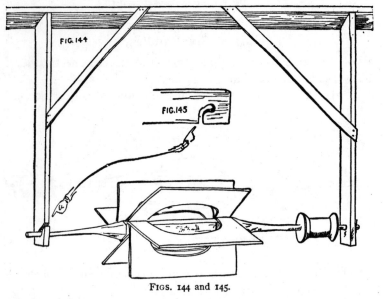

FIGS. 144 and 145.

one hanging-bar, and a hole is bored near the end of the
opposite hanging-bar.

To adjust the wheel, place the top bar across the bath-
tub and then slip the shaft in the hole in the hanging-bar,

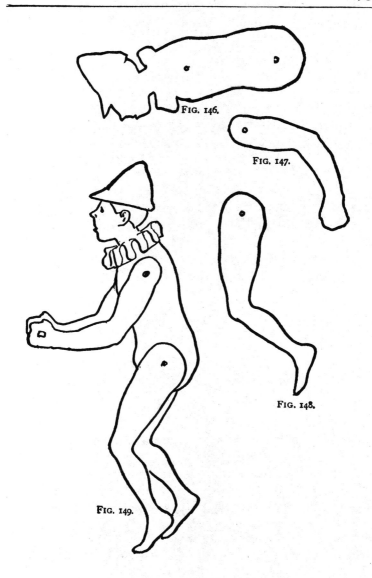

Fig. 146.

Fig. 147.

Fig. 148.

Fig. 149.

sliding the other end of the shaft into the slot shown in Fig. 145.

If the water is now allowed to run slowly from the faucet and fall upon the inside paddles it will set the

The Circus Performers.

wheel in motion, and this motion can be transmitted to any small and simple piece of machinery by means of a belt running from the spool which is attached to the wheel to a similar spool, attached to the machine.

If you Make a Frame,

similar to that which holds the water-wheel, (Fig. 144) and make it with much shorter hanging-bars, it will not be necessary to support them with the diagonal pieces. This second frame can be reversed over the first frame, so that the hanging-bars will set upright upon the cross-bar, and when in that position a small horizontal bar may be made to revolve by connecting a spool placed upon this bar with the spool upon the wheel-shaft, by means of a string loop. If this string is not too loose, nor yet too tight, it will turn

the top spool as soon as the water sets the wheel and the
bottom spool in motion. The illustration on page 196 shows
how a number of funny animals and men can be made to
do circus tricks on the bar, to the great delight of the
spectators.

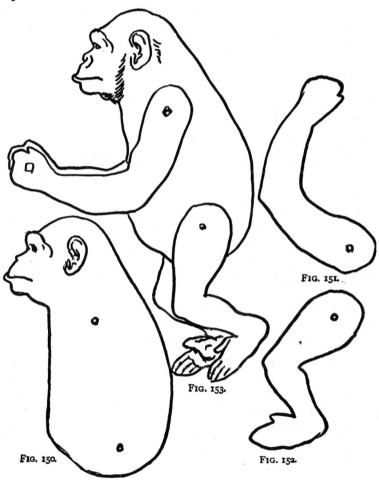

FIG. 151.

FIG. 153.

FIG. 150.

FIG. 152.

Figures Which Move.

To make these figures so that they will move with comical, but natural, movements, place a piece of transparent paper over the diagrams and trace the outlines, then blacken another piece of paper, upon one side, with a soft pencil; next place a piece of clean card-board under these figures, over the card-board spread the paper, with the blackened side next to the card-board, and over this put the tracing paper, and then, holding it so that it will not slip, follow the lines of the clown, ape, and donkey, with the point of a hard pencil. When the card-board is removed the bodies of the clown, ape, and donkey will appear traced upon the white surface.*

In the same manner make tracings of the legs and arms of the puppets, and with your scissors cut these figures out. Using the legs and arms cut from the card-board as patterns, trace around each of them upon another piece of card-board with a pencil, and cut these duplicates out. You will now have two each of Figs. 147, 148, 151, 152, 155 and 156.

With the point of your hard pencil, or a darning-needle, punch holes in all these parts, at the points marked by black dots.

Next take a small piece of string and make

A Neat, Round Knot

in one end of it, and thread the other end through the clown's arm, at the dot in his shoulder; then thread the string through the dot in the clown's body, near his collar (Fig. 146). Now thread through the hole in the shoulder of the duplicate arm. When this much is done, place the

---

* Another plan is described in Chapter XXIV.

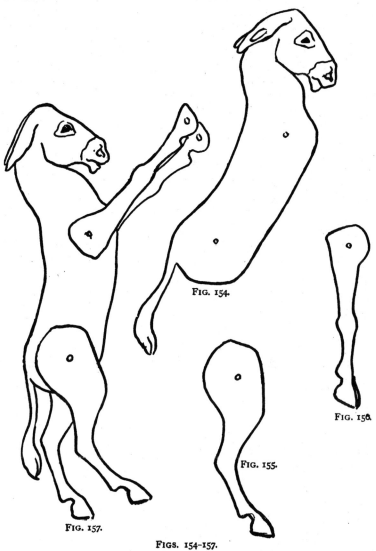

Fig. 154.

Fig. 155.

Fig. 156.

Fig. 157.

Figs. 154–157.

clown upon a table, with the knot underneath, and drawing the string up, while holding the clown's body down with your other hand, bring the knot snugly against the lower arm and tie another knot tightly against the upper arm. This last knot can be made by making a large loop, and then holding the string in place with one finger until the knot is slid down against the pasteboard arm and drawn tightly in place; a second and third knot, tied over this, will make it large enough for the purpose, and the arms will be found to move freely, up or down (See Fig. 289, Chapter XXIV.).

Attach the legs in the same manner; if you will now thrust a small stick through both the clown's fists you can make him take all the positions of a trained circus-man, by twirling the horizontal stick between your fingers.

When the water-wheel sets the bar twirling, the donkey, ape, and clown go through their "stunts," in a most laugh. able manner.

CHAPTER XVII.

GOOD GAMES WITH TOOTHPICKS AND MATCHES.

THE genuine American lad needs no costly toys with which to amuse himself, for he has inherited from a long

FIG. 158.—Rainy Day Fun.

line of pioneer ancestors a sturdy self-reliance. When the inclemency of the weather, or some slight illness, confines him to his home, he can pass away the time with toys of his own construction.

FIG. 159.—Toothpick Puzzle.

A Toy is a Plaything,

and a plaything is any old thing which chance throws in our way, with which to play.

Wooden Toothpicks

offer many opportunities for amusement. I have seen grown men, in the reading-rooms of our great hotels, amuse themselves and companions for hours with only a handful of wooden toothpicks.

Suppose that m u m p s have invaded the household, and the younger members of the family are, consequently, confined indoors, with their youthful jaws tied up in bandages. If they have no ingenuity they will be fretful and annoying to their parents and themselves, but if they have inherited true Yankee grit and invention they will spend their enforced imprisonment in a very jolly manner.

FIG. 160.—Solution.

Here is

A Simple Toothpick Example,

Fig. 159. Let us see you take away five toothpicks and leave three perfect squares.

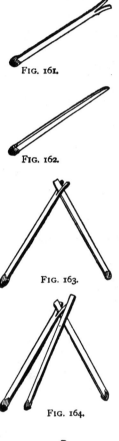

FIG. 161.

FIG. 162.

FIG. 163.

It is a simple problem, and one glance at Fig. 160 shows how it is done, but you must remember that the other fellows or girls to whom you put the question are not supposed to know the solution, and unless the puzzle-workers are very bright it will take some thinking to work out the problem—at least it will take enough thought to be a source of amusement to all concerned.

When the toothpicks are removed and the problem solved, ask them to

Lift Three Safety-Matches with One Toothpick.

Be sure to use safety-matches, if they are to be had; if not, use burnt matches, for there is no fun playing with toys which are liable to ignite and cause much more serious results than a case of mumps.

FIG. 164.

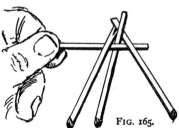

After all the party have tried in vain to lift the three matches with the aid of one toothpick, you may show them how the trick is done.

FIG. 165.

Explanation.

Fig. 161 shows the first match, which has been split at the tail-end with the blade of a pocket-knife; Fig. 162 shows another match, which has had the tail-end whittled to a wedge-shaped edge, and Fig. 163 shows the two matches joined by forcing the wedge end of one match into the split end of the other. Fig. 164 shows the third match, placed across the ends of the other two matches.

If you will now pass the toothpick under the first two matches and over the last, as illustrated by the diagram, Fig. 164, it is a simple task to lift the three matches and show your playmates how a seemingly impossible proposition becomes a thing of great simplicity when it is solved (Fig. 165.)

A Spring-Bed.

Now take a toothpick, Fig. 166, and place another one across it, as in Fig. 167; cross these two toothpicks, in their

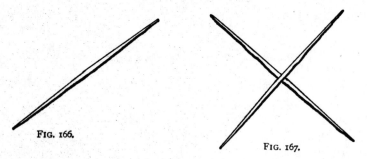

FIG. 166.

FIG. 167.

centre, with a third, as in Fig. 168; then run a fourth under the ends of the two side toothpicks and over the end of the middle one, as in Fig. 169.

When the fifth toothpick is run under the other ends of

the two crossed picks and over the free end of the centre toothpick, you will have Fig. 170.

What is Fig. 170? Well, it is almost anything you wish:

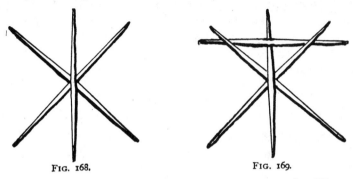

Fig. 168.   Fig. 169.

it is a gate, a section of a fence, or a spring-bed. Fig. 171 shows the spring-bed, and to prove that it is a real spring-bed, if you will set it on the hearth, where there can be no danger from fire, you may light one leg of the bed with a

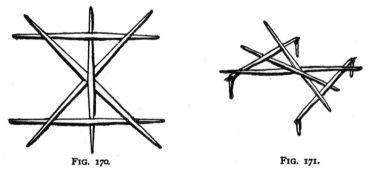

Fig. 170.   Fig. 171.

match, then stand back and watch the flame eat its way to the first joint. When this joint is reached the spring is freed, and the bed flies to pieces, which proves that it is really a spring-bed.

Artificial Water.

If you wish something to represent water, take a small looking-glass and place it flat on the floor or a table. Upon the surface of your glass lake you can place paper boats, and build shores by heaping books around the edge. Spanning the water you may have a beautiful bridge of toothpicks or safety-matches.

A Bridge of Matches.

This bridge requires patience and deft fingers to build, but both patience and skill are necessary in golf, football,

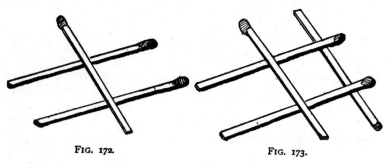

FIG. 172.   FIG. 173.

boating, the school, the counting-house, and in art or music, so you must not be discouraged if your frail match bridge falls to pieces just when you think the thing is about finished. Remember that an occasional failure is more than half the fun; start over again by placing two matches on the table and placing a third match across them, as in Fig. 172; then another match under them, as in Fig. 173. Some matches are made of such brittle stuff as to be unsuited for this, and others are too short and thick to bend, but good slender matches can be used, and wooden toothpicks are even better.

Fig. 174 shows the next step is to thrust two matches under the under match and over the match which is on top and across the first two; the spring in the matches will hold this frame to- gether. More and more matches may be added, in the same manner as the first (Fig. 175), until the arch is of the required length: that is, until it is long

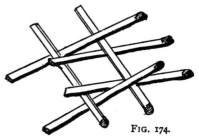

Fig. 174.

enough to reach from shore to shore of the looking-glass lake.

If you will now build

Two Piers,

or abutments, of matches, by placing a couple of sticks on each side of the water for the foundations—the two sticks to be parallel with each other—and two more across the ends of these, log-cabin fashion, until the piers are about two inches high, facing each other from opposite sides of the looking-glass, you may set your arch across, from pier to pier.

Two Approaches to the Bridge

must now be built, in the same manner as the arch, so that the arch can be reached from the shore (Fig. 176), and you will then have a pretty little structure, spanning a calm and dainty sheet of water.

If you are still not satisfied with the results of your skill, you may

Add a Roof

to each of your bridge piers, by erecting sides made on the pattern of Fig. 170, and either capping them with a paper roof or log-cabin built pyramids, composed of pieces of matches of different lengths, growing smaller toward the top.

A Paper Flag,

upon the end of a broom-straw, will add dignity and effect to your bridge; erect it by thrusting the lower end of the flag-staff through the roof and pier.

Tiring of bridges and puzzles, you can lay out

A Pioneer Settlement,

and with toothpicks and matches build log-cabins, such as those in which our ancestors lived when this land was covered with vast forests of trees and populated with painted Indians and wild beasts. Roof your houses with cards bent in the shape of a roof, and build your chimneys at one end of the house.

The Chimneys

in all log-cabins are built outside and against one end of the house, and are usually made of sticks and mud, or stones and mud; but as the rooms in an ordinary dwelling or flat furnish neither stones nor clay, you must do as our ancestors did: use the material at hand; which, in your case, will probably be spools from your mother's work-basket. Set the spools, one on top of another, against the end of your match-stick house and your work is done.

Not only is your work done, but, if you have followed all these directions, probably the day is also done, and you are ready for bed and to dream of living in safety-match houses near the shores of a looking-glass lake; and as you listen you will hear the glass waves breaking on the shore, and the howl of the toothpick timber-wolves as they steal among the rocky crags, made of spelling-books, arithmetics and dictionaries; or you may be startled from your sleep by the crack of a match-gun and the answering boom of a spool-cannon; but these things will only make your sleep the more peaceful and refreshing.

FIGS. 175 and 176.—The Toothpick Bridge.

CHAPTER XVIII.

FUN WITH SCISSORS AND PASTEBOARD AND PAPER.

In winter there are always some blustering, windy days, when the raw winds from off the ocean howl through our streets, making the lives of pedestrians miserable; or days when slush and sleet cause us to wish that we could stay in the house until winter was packed away in last year's almanac.

During such weather there is no fun to be had outdoors, and we must look for our amusement inside the four walls of our homes.

It is not every city boy who has an old-fashioned attic to romp in during bad weather, nor even a basement where he can seek to amuse himself building sleds or other outdoor appliances, for use when the weather will permit.

Many lads are confined in the narrow rooms of flats, and must needs fret and worry when the bad weather imprisons them in their narrow home-quarters.

But if such boys will stop quarrelling among themselves, and cease for a moment teasing the cat, or in other ways adding to the worries of their dear mamma, they may, by following the directions given here, find amusement and fun—not only for this particular bad day, but for all the stormy weather of the winter.

How to Make the Sleigh.

Fold a card or a piece of card-board in the middle, and with a pair of shears cut a curved piece off one end, as in Fig. 177.

Now take a sharp penknife and cut along the black lines

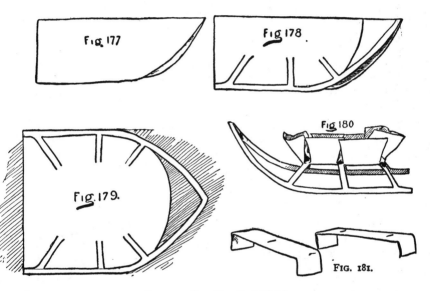

FIGS. 177–181.—The Card Sleigh.

of Fig. 178. When you spread out the card you will have Fig. 179, and if you bend up all the flaps and bend down the runners, giving the latter a pinch where they meet in the centre, you will have as dainty a little sleigh as old Santa Claus ever owned (Fig. 180).

The seats to the sleigh are simply made, being two strips of card-board with the corners bent down (Fig. 181).

How to Make the Horses.

The horses are more difficult to make, especially for boys who do not know how to draw a horse; but if such

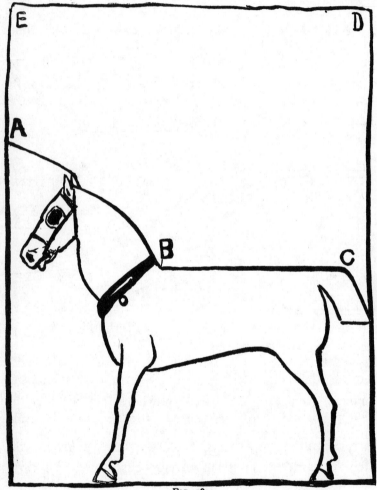

FIG. 182.

youngsters will read the preceding chapter it will tell them how to make a tracing, and they may make an exact reproduction of this horse by reversing the tracing and placing a clean piece of card-board underneath it, and then, with a lead-pencil, drawing over all the lines as they are in the illustration. When the card-board is removed they will find a faint outline of the horse upon the card-board.

To Cut Out the Horse,

commence at A (Fig. 182), and cut down to B; then fold the card-board carefully along the line of the back of the horse, BC.

BC will now be the top fold and ED will be down to the feet of the horse, while AB will stand up above the back, because AB has not been folded.

The rest is not hard work, for any child can follow the outline with the scissors, and the result will be a paper horse with four legs, upon which it can stand (Fig. 183).

Figs. 184, 185, and 186 can be traced in the same manner as the horse, and afterward cut out, leaving a pointed piece of card-board hanging down, which we

FIG. 183.—The Paper Horse.

stick through slits cut in the seats (Fig. 181), and in this manner make the driver and the passengers sit firmly in the sleigh.

The Tongue, or Pole.

A small, smooth stick will answer for the pole to the sleigh, and it may be fastened with a piece of thread to the

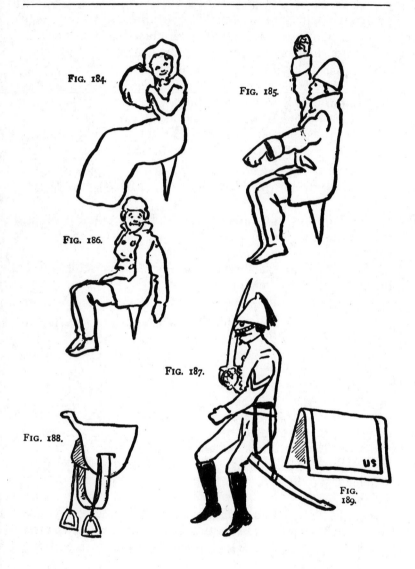

FIG. 184.

FIG. 185.

FIG. 186.

FIG. 187.

FIG. 188.

FIG. 189.

centre of a wooden toothpick which has been previously
thrust through the front runners of the sleigh, as in Fig.
191. The harness and reins are
simply strings tied to wooden
whiffletrees and run through holes
punched in the horses at the
proper places.

A broom-straw, pushed through
a hole in the driver's hand, will
do service for a whip, and you
may now have a grand spiked
team of five horses, if you choose
to make that number, or a simple two-horse or even one-horse
sleigh, as you may choose to make

FIG. 190.

it: the number of horses being limited only by the industry
of their creators.

The Pasteboard Soldiers.

For a bold soldier man, make the horse just as you made
the sleigh horse, but a cavalryman needs a saddle, and if
you cut out the protruding front of the saddle first and then

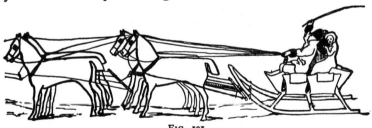

FIG. 191.

fold it as you did with the horse, you may make a saddle
similar to Fig. 188. The girth and stirrups are put on after
the saddle is cut out, the girth being a band of ribbon run

through slits in the saddle and fastened around the paper horse.

The Stirrups

are cut out of card-board, and fastened to the saddle with short strings. The saddle-cloth, Fig. 189, is a piece of paper, folded as shown in the diagram.

192

Trace the soldier, Fig. 187, in the manner already described, then cut him out and set him upon his saddled charger.

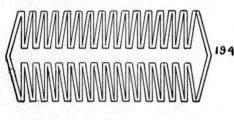

193

Make reins of string and run the string through a hole punched in the horse's mouth —where the bit should be— and through a hole punched in the soldier's hand. Put the cavalryman's feet in the paste-board stirrups and you have Fig. 190—a bold soldier man, ready for a parade, or to fight with the English or against them.   In fact, so perfect a soldier and

Such an Ideal Soldier

is this pasteboard man, that he will never question your orders, but fight on any side you choose to put him, and when he is worn out in the service he will utter no complaint if he is buried in the waste-paper basket, or even used for the purpose of kindling the kitchen fire.

Make an Army.

If you are successful in making one soldier, with industry you may make a whole regiment of them, and then stand them in battle array and shoot them down with a pea-shooter.

Your conscience need not bother you in the least, if you slay a whole regiment, for the poor fellows won't care a cent, and they will leave no widows and orphans behind to mourn for them. In fact, you can bring them all to life again, the next time you want a battle, by simply setting them upright upon their horses once more.

It sometimes happens that boys tire of soldiers and their murderous weapons, although both the soldier and his arms be but harmless paper.

At such a time the reader can put away his paper warriors and proclaim to his playmates that he is a wizard, and can

Walk through the Centre of a Visiting Card.

He may prove that this is no vain boast by folding the card, Fig. 192, across its centre (Fig. 193), and with scissors cutting slits where the lines are drawn on Fig. 193.

When the card is unfolded it will be found to resemble

Fig. 194, and may be stretched carefully until it can be passed over the head, down over the body to the feet; then as the self-proclaimed wizard steps out of the card he may truthfully say that he has walked through a visiting card.

After this he may entertain his playmates by making a

Grandmother's Reticule

of a square piece of paper (Fig. 195), which he folds at the dotted centre line (Fig. 196), and folds again across its centre (Fig. 197). The next fold is a diagonal one, from corner to corner (Fig 198).

With the scissors he cuts Fig. 198, as shown by the ruled lines on Fig. 199.

Carefully unfolding the paper he puts a marble or some other weight in the centre, which stretches the paper to the form of a paper reticule, Fig. 200.

FIG. 200.

Speaking of grandmothers reminds us of old times, when above the open grate fireplace the mantel and panelling was painted a sombre black.

The boys then used to amuse themselves by folding pieces of paper in the form of Fig. 198, and then cutting

"Any Old Thing"

out with the scissors—the result being that when the

paper was unfolded the meaningless "thing" resolved itself into a beautiful geometrical pattern, which showed to great advantage when stuck upon the black woodwork of the mantel.

Benjamin Franklin, Benjamin Harrison, and Thomas Lynch, Jr., were appointed a committee by the Continental Congress to design a national flag for the baby United States, and you all know that in the little old house, 239 Arch Street, Philadelphia, Betsey Ross made the

First American Flag.

You have also probably read the legend so frequently published, which tells us that the stars in the original design were six-pointed, and were only changed because some one showed how

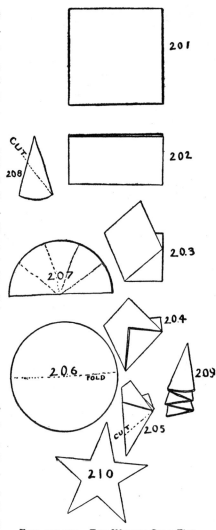

FIGS. 201–210.—Two Ways to Cut a Five-pointed Star.

To Cut a Five-pointed Star with One Clip of the Scissors,

by folding Fig. 201 in the form of Fig. 202, and folding the latter in the form of Fig. 204, again folding in the shape of Fig. 205, and then making a cross-cut at the dotted line. When the paper was unfolded it appeared in the form of Fig. 210, a five-pointed star.

Another Way to Cut a Five-pointed Star,

is to fold a circular disk of paper (Fig. 206) across its diameter (Fig. 207), and fold this in the form of a fan (Fig. 209),

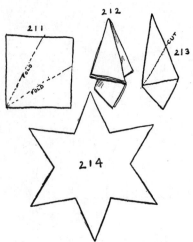

which when pressed down flat will be Fig. 208. One cut, where the dotted line is shown on Fig. 208, will produce the five-pointed star (Fig. 210). If, as according to the legend, it was because of the simplicity of this one clip of the scissors that the five-pointed star was adopted, the old legend needs revision, for

A Six-pointed Star can be made with One Cut,

FIGS. 211–214.—A Six-pointed Star, with One Cut.

with no more trouble than it takes to make the five-point.

Fold the paper as in Figs. 195, 196, and 197 (see Reticule). Fold the form (Fig. 197) fan-wise, at the dotted lines on Fig. 211, making the divisions equal (Fig. 212). Press the folds down until they are flat (Fig. 213), and make the cut at the place indicated by the dotted line. When the paper is unfolded you will have the six-pointed star, Fig. 214.

This is the star of the East, which guided the wise men to the lowly manger—the Star of Bethlehem, a grander and better symbol than the irregular five-pointed star. The six-pointed star stands for Peace on Earth, Good Will to Men. The magicians of old called the six-pointed star the "pentacle" of Solomon.

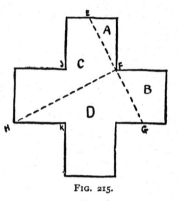

Fig. 215.

One of the oldest and most venerated symbols is

The Cross,

and if you make one of the proportions of five squares, each of the three arms of equal size, and equal to the square space in the middle, you may, by

Two Cuts, make the Cross into a Square.

This will, at first glance, look like an impossibility, but if

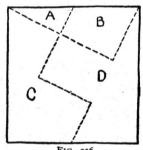

Fig. 216.

you find the middle of the top end of the cross (Fig. 215), and lay a straight-edge from the middle point E, touching the corner F, and rule the line E F G, then rule a line from H to F, and cut where the lines are ruled, you will have four irregular pieces, A, B, C, and D, which you may fit together in the form of a square (Fig. 216).

This is amusement enough for one rainy day, and for the next one you may try something more artistic, and consequently more difficult and interesting.

CHAPTER XIX.

HOW TO PREPARE AND GIVE A BOYS' CHALK-TALK.

A NATURAL taste or talent for art is almost universal. If any of my readers doubt this statement let them supply all the youngsters in their neighborhood with colored chalks and note the result.

My word for it, there will not be a paving-flag, wall or fence in the ward, which offers an opportunity for a picture, which will not be profusely decorated with brilliantly colored, grotesque figures.

We are all Born Artists.

The truth is that the ability and desire to draw, come just as natural to a child as its ability and desire to talk.

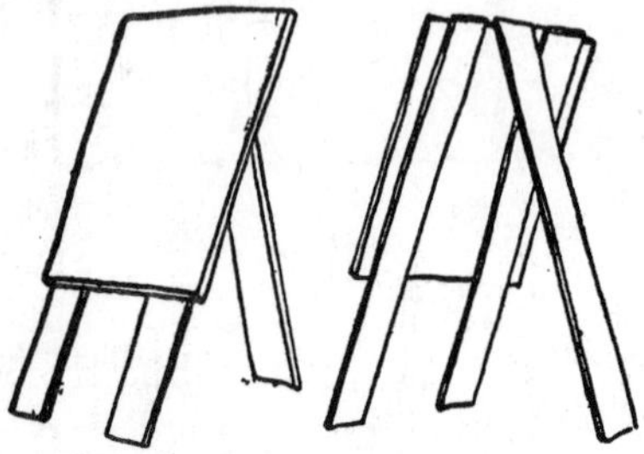

FIGS. 217 and 218.—The Drawing-board.

That almost all children learn to talk with more or less fluency, while few learn to draw with any approach to skill, is because talking is encouraged and systematically taught from earliest infancy, while drawing is discouraged, and has been ever since the days of old Sakya-Muni, 400 years before the Christian era. Sakya, the narrow-minded old heathen, thought it detrimental to progress in virtue to waste one's time with pencil or brush.

And to-day, in the gray light of the dawn of the twentieth century, boys are often forbidden to draw and few are encouraged in the practice, so that, in fear of punishment, the youngsters give vent to their artistic feelings by slyly decorating the flags, walls, and fences.

FIG. 219.—A Chalk-Talker.

Art will never reach the proper standard until these little "chalk-talkers" are encouraged, and taught to handle their chalk with the same skill with which they are taught to use their tongues.

The Name Chalk-Talk

was invented by Frank Beard, D.D., the veteran cartoonist, lecturer, and college professor, and it is the title of his first public lecture, but since then it has grown to be a popular

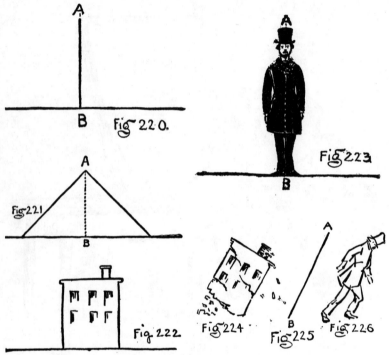

FIGS. 220-226.—The Character of Lines.

name, so that whenever a speaker illustrates what he has to say by pictures, drawn before the audience, the entertainment is called a chalk-talk.

Besides the ability to stand before an audience and talk, it is absolutely necessary to have some little knowledge of drawing, before one can hope to make a success in this field.

However, any lad, with ordinary ability, can

Learn by Practise

to draw well enough to give an interesting show, suitable for the school-room, Sunday-school, or for a drawing-room entertainment.

For this a good blackboard and a few colored chalks are all the material necessary. The blackboard is a most ex-

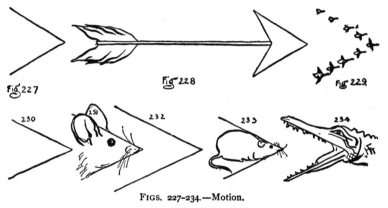

FIGS. 227-234.—Motion.

cellent thing upon which to practise, but it is much better to use large sheets of yellowish-brown paper. This paper is known as chalk-talk paper, and has "tooth" enough to retain the chalk, and make every stroke tell.

Figs. 217 and 218 show how to make a

Drawing-Board,

upon which to fasten the paper. Fig. 217 shows the front view. Fig. 218 the rear view. The drawing-board can be made of any size to suit the artist, but should always be large enough to give full sweep to the arm.

Size of Board.

To get these proportions take a piece of charcoal in your hand and stand at arm's length from the wall, with your right side toward it, and without changing your position, or leaning forward, make a mark as high upon the wall as you can reach. In the same manner make a mark as low as you can reach, without stooping. Swing your arm from left to right, make two marks midway between and upon each side of the first marks. This will give you the full extent of your reach. It is well to allow a foot more, each way, for a margin. This will give the proper proportion for the drawing-board.

The board must be made of soft, smooth pine boards, so matched that there will be no cracks to annoy you while drawing.

The Height of the Easel

can be obtained by measuring from the floor to the top mark on the wall, and allowing a foot more for the margin.

The easel is made by screwing two leg-boards on the back of the drawing-board (Fig. 217), and then, with a hinge in the middle of the top edge of the drawing-board, attaching the third or hind leg (Fig. 218).

Tack the Paper

securely, at the top and bottom, to the drawing-board, spread your colored chalks out on the table, and group the colors so that they will be handy, and when you want any color you will waste no time seeking that particular lump of chalk (Fig. 219).

Keep a Sharp Knife

handy, on the table, so that as soon as the audience has seen one picture you can run the point of the knife along the bottom of the paper, just above the tacks, free the lower edge of the drawing, throw it up and over the top of the easel, without taking time to detach it at the top. You are then ready to begin upon a new drawing.

The Drawings Themselves

must be simple, but with practice some very effective designs can be made with a few rapid strokes, which at a distance will look like finished paintings. You may

Begin Your Talk

by drawing a vertical line AB (Fig. 220). As soon as this is done you must *step aside, so that all the audience may see*

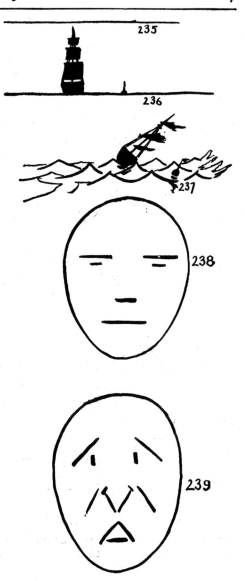

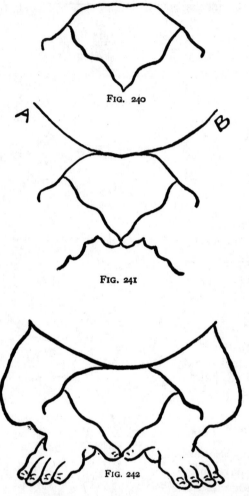

FIG. 240

A   B

FIG. 241

FIG. 242

what you have drawn, and while they are looking at the
line tell them that you are going to give them a talk upon
the character of lines, and what the lines represent.

AB conveys the idea of

A Stationary Object

—a telegraph pole, a tree, a church steeple, etc.   If there is one idea which it does not suggest, that idea is motion.

Draw two lines diagonally down from A to the base line (Fig. 221), and point out that this represents a pyramid, which when resting upon its base is the

Emblem of Stability.

Upon another sheet of paper draw two **AB** lines, and

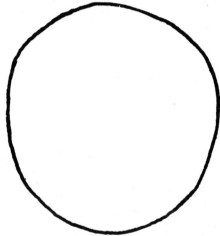

FIG. 243.

joining them at the top (Fig. 222), show that these lines still represent a stationary object—a house.

At this point you may work in any comic story of houses in a Western tornado, which, under a stress of weather are not stationary, but seem inclined to change their base and even to fly, etc.   Fig. 243 shows how a man becomes a stationary object when the line AB divides him in the centre.

Motion.

But when you slant the AB lines they suggest motion
(Figs. 224, 225, and 226).

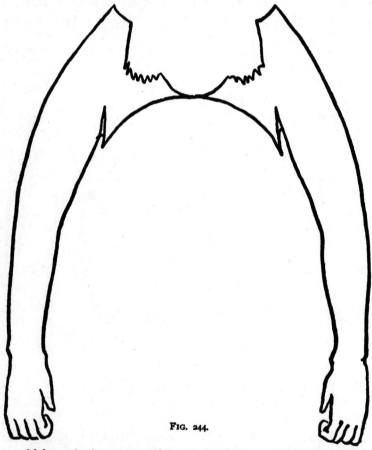

FIG. 244.

Although the pyramid is the emblem of stability, when
resting upon its base—with the AB line dividing it in the
centre—if you take the same form and point the apex in any

other direction it immediately suggests motion, as in Figs.
227, 228, and 229.

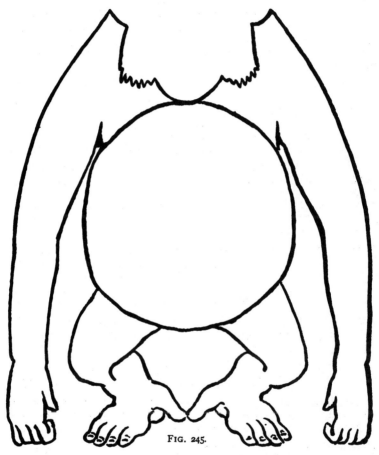

FIG. 245.

Not only does it suggest motion, but it tells the direction of the movement suggested. Any child can tell in
which direction the arrow and the ducks are flying.

There is

Another Meaning

to this figure. It is a wedge, and means cleaving—entering into—(Figs. 230, 231, 232, and 233). But when one views it from the opposite direction the meaning is just the opposite to a wedge. It now means reception (Fig. 234). The mouse is entering and the alligator is receiving.

Draw All Your Figures as Large as the Paper Will Permit

you to make them; otherwise the audience, or some persons in the back part of the audience, will miss part of your talk, and that will spoil their enjoyment and diminish your applause.

Upon a new sheet of paper draw a horizontal line (Fig. 235), and explain that

This Line Means Repose.

It is the position a person assumes in sleep · it is the surface of the ocean during a calm (Fig. 236).

Here we again have the upright line AB (of Fig. 220), in the mast of the becalmed and immovable ship of Fig. 236. When a squall comes up not only does AB change to a diagonal line (Fig. 237), but the horizontal line, indicating repose, is broken into a series of irregular points, showing noise, movement, and commotion. Figs. 238 and 239 show the same effect of lines.

Something Which Needs Practice,

is the ape; but when you draw it carefully a few times and then practise on it, as you would upon a difficult feat in

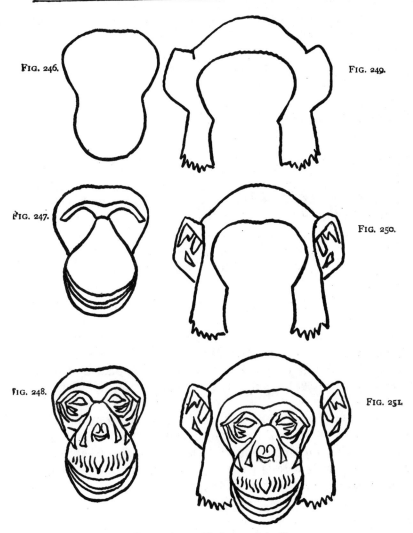

FIG. 246.

FIG. 247.

FIG. 248.

FIG. 249.

FIG. 250.

FIG. 251.

FIGS. 246–251.—Evolution of the Face.

skating, or any other sport, you can learn to draw the thing in less than a minute.   The

Evolution of the Ape

is its growth from a few simple lines.   First draw Fig. 240, then add a curved line to the top of the first figure and some wiggles to the bottom (Fig. 241).

A few more strokes of the chalk and we have the comical short legs, long toes, and big thumbs (Fig. 242).   Prolong the curve which you drew upon top of the legs until you have an irregular circle (Fig. 243), and on top of the circle fit Fig. 244, the arms of the ape.   Make the knuckles rest upon the ground, each side of the feet.   From Fig. 246 to Fig. 251, inclusive, is the evolution of the face; but

For Quick Work

most all of the wrinkles shown in Figs. 248 and 251 may be left out.   Simply draw the nose and eyes upon Fig. 247 and add the ears, hair, and whiskers (Fig. 250), and it will look ape-like enough to bring applause.   When this is finished you have the late lamented Mr. Crowley, of Central Park Zoo (Fig. 252), which will gain sufficient applause to fully repay you for all the time spent in practising on the evolution of the ape.

This will be enough for one talk, and if interlarded with amusing stories and narrations, will not only hold and amuse your audience, but will teach them some real truths in the sign language of drawing, and give them the beginner's lesson in the meaning of lines.

FIG. 252.—Mr. Crowley.

CHAPTER XX.

A CHRISTMAS NOVELTY FOR BOYS.

How to Build and Decorate a Fireplace for Santa Claus.

To Mr. Clement C. Moore we are indebted for the creation of that jolly little gnome, the Americanized Santa Claus, Kris Kringle, or Saint Nicholas. When "The Night Before Christmas" was written our homes all possessed ample chimneys and spacious fireplaces, affording a most convenient entrance for the merry little saint; but now he is without doubt sorely puzzled by our modern houses, and experiences great discomfort and difficulty in entering the hot-air chamber of the furnaces, and squeezing his corpulent little body and his pack of gifts through the registers.

A deep sense of gratitude for many favors received, induces me to offer a few suggestions which will help the friend of my boyhood to come, as of old, through the chimney.

Fig. 253 shows

The First Start

for the framework, which is made of smooth or rough pine strips, ½ inch thick by 2 inches in width. Make the frame about 5 feet 4 inches high by 4 feet 6 inches wide; the top and lower pieces 4 feet 5 inches (A, B, and C, D, Fig. 253) long, thus allowing ½ inch at each end, to fit the ends of the side-pieces (R and S, Fig. 256). The diagonals, X and Y (Fig. 253), are temporary braces, to keep the frame in shape, and are nailed at each end in such a manner that the nails may be easily withdrawn when it is necessary. The illustration is so clear that there should be no difficulty in following its lines.

FIG. 253.—Beginning the Framework.

The frame, A, E, F, B (Fig. 254), is the

Back of the Chimney,

and should reach to the ceiling of the room in which the fireplace is to be built. Set the frame, A, B, C, D (Fig. 253), against the wall; then take Z (Fig. 254) and raise it up until it touches the ceiling, and drive a nail at the intersection of X and Y into Z, and another exactly in the centre of A, B; drive them far enough to hold Z in an upright position, but leave enough of the nail-heads protruding to make it easy to redraw them and remove the temporary braces, X, Y, and Z (Fig. 254), when the whole frame will be finished and ready to use.

FIG. 254.—The Back of the Chimney.

Take a stick half the length of A, B (E, F, Fig. 254), and nail the end of Z exactly to the centre of E, F. By pushing up one end or the other you may put E, F exactly at right

angles, or " square " with Z.   When the stick, E, F, is found
to be square, cut two more sticks, A, E and F, B, each a
trifle longer than the distance from A to E; cut the ends of
these sticks to fit on the top of A, B, and "toe-nail" them
in place, as is shown in the small diagram in the upper right-
hand corner of Fig. 254.   Allow the upper ends of A, E, and
F, B to slip under the ends of the stick, E, F, as in the illustration, and nail them securely in place; then saw off the
protruding ends even with E, F, and the back of your frame
is finished.

The Front Frame

(Fig. 255) is of the same width as A, B, Fig. 253, but it is
the width of the strips R and S, Fig. 256 (two inches),
shorter than the back.   The side-pieces, G, N, and H, Q
(Fig. 255), are set with their edges facing the front, and the
top-piece, G, H (Fig. 255), is fitted in with its broad surface
facing the front and flush with the tops and front edges of
the side-pieces, G, N, and H, Q; it is held in place by nails
driven through the side-pieces in the ends of G, H.

The piece J, K, is exactly the same length as G, H, and
forms the top of the fireplace, but unlike G, H, the piece
J, K, has its thin edge flush with the front.   It is held in
place by nails which are driven through from the outside
of the two uprights, G, N, and H, Q.   All these pieces must
be cut and fitted with exactness, or the framework will be
of no use.

Fig. 256 shows how

The Remaining Pieces,

LO, MP, NO, and PQ, are placed, and the figure of the
young workman gives an idea of their proportions which
cannot be given in figures, for the reason that the opening

for the fireplace must be made to suit the size of the boy who is to be Santa Claus.

To finish the framework is now

FIG. 255.—The Front Frame.

A Simple Task.

Make two bottom side-bars (C, N, and D, Q, Fig. 256), each about two and one-half feet long, and nail them in place, " toe-nailing " at the front. The two top-bars (R and S, Fig. 256) must extend out a foot in front, as a support for

the mantel-piece.   After these are securely nailed in p ace
the roof-sticks, **a** and **d,** may be fitted in place, and notched
to fit over the mantel supports, as shown in Fig. 256.   You
now have a strong but light frame, which must be neatly

FIG. 256.—The Finished Frame.

covered with gray-colored paper muslin, Manila paper, or building paper.

The Covering

must be stretched, and securely tacked to the framework, so that no wrinkles shall betray its frail nature.

Some black paper muslin is now needed

To Line the Inside of the Fireplace.

Tack the ends of two pieces of the black stuff on the uprights, LO, and MP, and extend one piece back to B, D, and the other to A, C, and tack them to the back frame; also stretch a piece of black muslin from A, C, to B, D. This will make the interior of the fireplace dark and mysterious.

Next take a pot of white paint and a small brush, and rule white horizontal lines all around the fireplace and chimney; then paint upright lines, as shown in the illustration (Fig. 257). This will give the effect of stonework with white plaster between.

Place a smooth board upon the projecting supports, R and S, for the mantel, and the work will be done. If you can secure some old-fashioned brass candlesticks and an antique clock, for your mantel, they will add greatly to the effect. A pair of andirons, with some charred sticks of wood, will give a realistic touch which will win applause (Fig. 257).

Our American St. Nicholas

is a jovial little fellow, with a very red nose, white hair, white beard, short pipe, fur-trimmed clothes, and a little round belly—which shakes when he laughs, like a bowl full of jelly. Every youngster also knows that he comes in a little sleigh, drawn by eight tiny reindeer; but in spite of this universal knowledge among the children of America of Santa Claus' personal characteristics, the long-legged saint of Europe still fills our illustrated papers, each year as heretofore, and badly upholstered giants are made to

FIG 257.—Ready for Christmas.

stand for the saint in all the shop-windows, and frighten the children out of their seven senses. It is a fact that many of the little ones take these big ungainly giants for the ones which Jack the Giant-killer is supposed to have slain.

All American children love their little American Christmas saint, whose individuality was born with the verses beginning

> " It was the night before Christmas, and all through the house
> Not a creature was stirring, not even a mouse," etc.

Any boy who has a box of tools, and is at all clever at carpentry, may make a framework similar to the one shown in the preceding illustrations, but when it comes to preparing the

Costume for Jolly Old Santa Claus

he will more than likely find it convenient to call for some assistance from his sisters, though, of course, he will enjoy the whole thing better if he can make it a real surprise.

But it is not very difficult for the boys to make a good representation of St. Nick themselves.

The Coat.

When making his costume secure a dark-colored sack coat which is much too large for the proposed Santa Claus, and turn back the sleeves at the cuffs until they are the proper length for Santa Claus's arms. Stitch the cuffs lightly to the sleeves, to keep them in place. Turn up the bottom of the coat all around, making it the proper length for the little man, and stitch the skirt in place; then, to represent fur, use white cotton-batting and cover the turned-back cuffs and skirt with this material, so as to conceal the alterations. Upon the white trimmings sew little tags of black cotton.

Use a Fur Cap,

if you have one; if not, take any sort of a dark cloth one, and sew a piece of white cotton around the edge. Cover the legs, below the knees, with heavy woollen stockings and use big overshoes for the feet.

How to Put on the Clothes.

When the boy who is to represent the jolly old saint is ready to dress, let him put on the knickerbockers first and stuff the bottom end of a pillow in the front of the breeches; then put on the coat, and button and belt the pillow inside. This will give him a jolly big paunch; next put on the stockings and the overshoes. Then let some one gum a pair of big white cotton eyebrows to his forehead, using common mucilage for the purpose; also a long white cotton mustache and beard. Press these appendages to the face until the mucilage is dry. The finishing touch is made by painting the nose a bright red, and then the brave old saint will be ready to hide in the spacious chimney, to descend and greet the company when he receives the signal that the proper time has come for his appearance.

If the false chimney and fireplace are set up against an open door, Santa Claus may enter from the other room, and when he lets himself down over the black cloth back of the fireplace it will appear to the audience—at least, to all the little folks—as if he came down the chimney.

In case no doorway is handy a strong board shelf, built in the false chimney, will serve as a seat and a place of concealment for the saint until the clock on the mantel strikes the hour of twelve, which should be the signal for the immediate appearance of the little man.

The Clock,

of course, should be set ahead of time, so that it will strike at the proper moment, when everything is in readiness, and the little folks are trembling with impatience.

CHAPTER XXI.

HOW TO MAKE TWO BOYS INTO ONE SANTA CLAUS.

IF your time for preparation is limited, and you still wish to have a live Santa Claus, you may do so by dispensing with the artificial fireplace altogether, and allowing the old saint to hold a reception in the doorway between two rooms.

The accompanying illustrations show you how you can make another real live Santa Claus, in your own home. Many of you are familiar with the trick of the so-called German dwarf, and this Santa Claus is an adaptation of that trick for a Christmas entertainment.

The first picture (Fig. 258) shows

FIG. 258.—Legs.

FIG. 259.—Legs with Coat.

How the Old Saint's Legs are Made

by pulling a pair of golf stockings over the hands and arms, and then slipping the hands into the slippers.

It is necessary to choose a short coat, for otherwise the tails would hide the feet. With any old fur, or substitute which will look like fur, trim the coat, making it appear as if it buttoned up in the middle of the back.

Some one then puts the coat, "wrong-side fore," on to the boy who acts as legs (Fig. 259).

The Wig and Beard

FIG. 260.—The Little Saint. Side-View.

are now put on Mr. Legs, and his nose is then painted a bright red, after which a peaked cap, made of some bright material and trimmed with something to represent fur, is placed upon his head.

"Mr. Legs" is now ready for "Mr. Arms," and the illustration (Fig. 260) shows Mr. Arms after he has thrust his hands and arms through the sleeves of the fur-trimmed coat.

The Curtains

are securely pinned behind Legs' head in front of Arms' face, and brought down around the fur-trimmed coat, outside of Legs' real legs, and pinned under his arms, which are doing the part of the saint's legs, thus concealing all but the little saint. The last illustration (Fig. 261) displays the jolly little saint distributing candy and small presents to the young people.

The more care you take in arranging your show, the greater will be the success of the entertainment. The eight little reindeer are not necessary, even if they were obtainable, for the old saint may be supposed to have unhitched his steeds for the time and stabled them on the roof; but

The Sleigh

can be improvised from any ordinary coasting-sled. Select one which looks something like a sleigh.

When fat little Santa Claus comes down the chimney, we all know that he carries his

Good Things in a Bag,

FIG. 261.—The Little Saint. Front View.

so if you secure a bag, and stuff it full of any sort of material, it will make a most appropriate load for the sleigh. A fur rug will add to the effect, but is not necessary.

If the sleigh and bag do not reach high enough for the saint to stand on, a stage must be made of some old box, covered by a white sheet or white canton-flannel cloth, to represent snow, and on this stage set the sleigh and bag, as shown in the illustration on page 250.

A second bag should be procured, in which all the presents have been placed; each present should be carefully covered with enough paper to protect it from injury, as well as to conceal and make a mystery of the contents of the package.

When All is Ready

have a curtain or screen set up before Santa Claus, turn down the lights and invite the company into the room, then make them keep very quiet and listen for Santa Claus.

In an adjoining room some one in the secret has a set of sleigh-bells, which are jingled very softly at first, gradually growing louder and louder, as if the sleigh was approaching nearer; when they stop a stamping of feet is heard.

This last is

The Signal for Legs,

who cries out, in his deepest bass, " A pretty Christmas this! Company here, and all hiding behind a screen. What, ho! are ye afraid of Santa Claus?" At that the master of ceremonies removes the screen, and there before the eyes of the delighted company is a real live Santa Claus, who can move his legs and arms, and talk!

The entertainment is

Concluded

by the old saint fishing the presents out of the bag and handing them to the master of ceremonies, who calls out the name found on each bundle and presents it to the claimant.

During the time devoted to the distribution of presents

Santa Claus can make plenty of fun, for as the arms belong to one boy and the legs and head to another, the legs and head never know exactly what the arms are about to do next, and if the arms take a handkerchief out of a pocket to wipe the face, there is always a mirth-provoking incident, and the face does not look happy until the handkerchief is put away.

CHAPTER XXII.

A CIRCUS IN THE ATTIC.

How to Make the Horses and Other Animals, and How to Make the Costumes.

In all mimic circus performances the boys of a generation ago were sadly handicapped by the want of horses; sometimes goats and dogs were pressed into service, but these animals flatly refused to allow the youthful circus riders to mount their backs, and as substitutes for horses proved good for nothing but the creation of confusion.

When

The Goat

was supposed to canter around the ring, he had a way of standing on his hind legs and coming down head-first, which utterly demoralized our ring-master, and even caused the clown to do many " stunts " not down on the programme. The dog would wag his tail and bark in a manner very unlike a true circus horse.

It sometimes happened that one of the performers was the proud owner of a real live pony. Alas! even a pony had its objectionable features, for however willing the animal might be to climb the stairs, for reasons unaccountable to us, our parents put forth such strong objections that the pony had to be left out of the show.

Since the Writer's Circus Days

the safety bicycle has made its appearance, and as a consequence every boys' show may now be supplied with circus

horses which the boys can ride, and which will neither butt
nor bark ; furthermore, parents will not object to the presence in the attic of rubber-shod hoofs, which make no noise.

The " Arab Steed "

is made by fastening a simple framework of sticks and
hoops to an ordinary wheel.   The head may be made of the

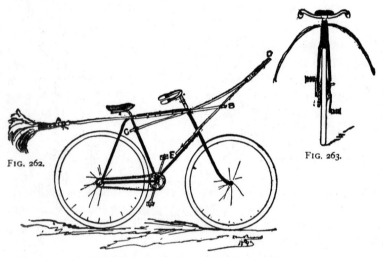

FIG. 262.   FIG. 263.

FIGS. 262 and 263.—Showing Skeleton of Horse.

canvas cover of a ham, stuffed with excelsior, or a piece of
cloth sewed into the form of a ham-cover, and stuffed lightly
with excelsior.

A Feather-Duster May Do Service as a Tail.

Fig. 262 shows the wheel, with the backbone rod, A B,
lashed to the top tube of the frame and the feather-duster
made fast to the tail-end of the rod, A B.

The Neck-Bones

are the two rods, C D and E D.   The rod C D is bound to
the saddle-post, below the point where the head and top
tubes join under the handle-bar.   The lower neck-bone, E

Fig. 264.—Ready for the Cover.

D, is lashed to the top of the bracket-tube at E, just out of
reach of the pedals, and to the upper neck-bone, at D.

The Ribs

are made from ordinary wooden barrel-hoops.   Fig. 263
shows front-view of wheel, with one hoop in place.   The first
hoop is tied on the neck-bone, in front of the handle-bars,
and the next two hoops are lashed to the backbone, behind

the saddle-bar, as shown in Fig. 264. The head is tied to the end of the neck-bones, at D, and eyes, mouth, and nostrils, painted on the ham-cover head.

The Frame

now only needs to be covered with a cloth of some kind, to make a most speedy "Arab steed." The covering for the

FIG. 265.

FIG. 266.

FIG. 267.

FIGS. 265-267.—The Inside of the Bird.

horse may be gaudily colored paper muslin, with the addition, perhaps, of some quaint figures cut out of gold, red, or black paper, and pasted in place, as shown by the illustration. Two sheets may be made to do duty as a horse-cover; or two old shawls, properly draped and fastened to the skeleton or framework, will answer the purpose; but it is, on the whole, best to buy the paper muslin, as this may be cut and sewed at pleasure. Cut it so as to cover both head and neck, leaving eye-holes and holes for mouth and nose, also a large opening where the fearless circus rider is to sit and work the pedals.

The Reins

may be made of ribbons and run from the mouth to the handle-bars. The horse's blanket should be stitched to the first hoop on the neck, and not allowed to hang loose, as it would be certain to interfere with the free movement of the front wheel and bring the Arab steed into trouble not down on the programme, causing him to act more like a bucking Western bronco than a gentle, well-trained circus horse.

The Moa is the Giant Bird from New Zealand,

and is simply made, as a glance at Figs. 265, 266, and 267 will prove.   Fig. 265 shows a cone made of card-board, the edges of which are stitched or glued together, and the whole covered with white or yellow paper.   Fig. 266 is the neck-bone, a stick with a pad of rags or paper tied over the upper end.   A sheet, or other plain-colored cloth, is stitched to the cone in such a manner that the drapery will fall down and hide all but the feet and legs of the boy holding the neck-bone (Fig. 267).   Some black paint or ink can be used to mark the eyes and mouth on the paper cone, and the only living example of the moa, the giant bird of New Zealand, is ready to be led around the ring before the eyes of the awe-struck spectators.   For an extra charge the strange bird will even allow one of the smaller spectators to ride its back (the boy's shoulders) around the ring.

The Manicora

is an imaginary beast, once thought to inhabit America. From all I can learn from old prints it was supposed to be a sort of lion, with a human face.   If any of your circus company own a French poodle, or any sort of long-haired dog which can be shaved like a lion, he can make a beautiful manicora by sewing a skirt, long enough to reach below the dog's collar, on to a cheap false-face.   With a lit-tle patient work the dog may be taught to walk around the ring with a false-face on.   The mask is held in place by tucking the cloth under the dog's collar.

By using

A Little Ingenuity,

any number of fierce and strange animals can be made, to

FIG. 268.

FIG. 269.

FIG. 270.

FIG. 271.

FIG. 272.

FIG. 273.

FIG. 274.

FIGS. 268–274.—Ring-master and His Costume.

astonish and please the audience; every boy knows how to
make an elephant of two boys covered with a gray shawl,

and a giraffe can be made by adding another boy to the moa, so as to give it four legs ; but the limited space at my disposal forbids my introducing more diagrams.

The Dignified and Self-sufficient Ring-master

must dress in black, and have high boots, or at least what appear to be high boots.   This appearance can be made with a few cents' worth of black paper muslin, sewed over two cylinders (Fig. 272) of pasteboard.   These, when finished, will look like top-boots (Figs. 273 and 274.)

Tight-fitting Knee-breeches,

black or some dark color, and a dark coat, will be all that is required for lower parts ; but the head must be adorned with a high hat, and if an old silk hat of the proper size cannot be procured, you can make one by fitting a muslin-covered pasteboard top on to an ordinary black derby hat (see Figs. 268, 269, 270, 271, and 274.)   A standing collar and a flashy or plain white necktie will finish the costume.   Of course the ring-master must have a long whip, with which he makes believe to whip the clown when the latter tries one of his jokes at the ring-master's expense.

A Jersey or a Tight-fitting Undershirt

will do duty for the circus rider's upper garment, and if he can induce some one to make him a pair of light-colored trunks he can appear in his underclothes, and no one will know but that he has on the regular showman's tights.

A Girl's Old Turban Hat,

set jauntily on his head, will add to the effect, especially if this head-gear be decorated with a long, curling feather.

Rainy Day Ideas.

FIG. 275.

FIG. 276.

FIG. 277.

I·AM· THE CLOWN

FIG. 278.

FIGS. 275–278.—The Clown.

If the reader is not fortunate in the possession of some accommodating female relative who will help him out by kindly making the trunks, he may take an old pair of loose-fitting

Knickerbockers,

and cut the legs off, just below the thigh ; then cut slits near the bottom, through which he may run a piece of tape, as the pucker-string is run in the top of a marble-bag.

To put on these trunks he must turn them

Wrong Side Out

and put them on upside down, then fasten the string as high up on his leg as it will go, after which he can reach down and turn the breeches up until they come to the proper place around his waist. It will then be seen that they are not only right side out, but that the cloth folds over and conceals the pucker-strings as neatly as if the trunks were made by a tailor.

Take an Old Soft Felt Hat

(Fig. 275) and soak it well in warm or hot water, then put it over the blunt end of a bedpost, or any similar object, and firmly but steadily pull down the rim (Fig. 276), until the crown is given a conical form (Fig. 277). If you pull too hard you will run the post through the hat ; but with a little care you may shape any old soft felt hat into the typical head-gear of the clown (Figs. 277, 278).

Your father's, big brother's, or uncle's

Pajamas,

will make an excellent suit of clothes for the clown. Hoist the pantaloons up under your arms and fasten them there ; then put garters around the ankles. Belt in the upper garments at the waist, and put elastic garters on your wrists. Persuade your sister, mother, or aunt, to make a ruff for your neck, from a piece of stiff white muslin, and you will have **as** good a clown's suit as appears in the real circus, (Fig. 278) When

Making-Up

for the ring, take some common flour and put it in a piece of mosquito-netting; with this, powder your hair, face, and neck, until all is as white as the driven snow, then **wet a** towel and mark out a big, laughing mouth.

You are now ready to caper into the ring and throw your peaked hat at the ring-master.

FIG. 279.—The Circus.

A BOYS' STAG-PARTY

CHAPTER XXIII.

THE only difference between the bald-headed, bearded boy and his younger brother in knickerbockers is that the latter is fond of fun and owns up to it, while the former is fond of fun and conceals the fact behind a solemn countenance and a severe and dignified frown.

But when the

Old Boys

attend a stag-party the solemn faces and frowns are not there; they leave them with their overcoats in the hall.

When sending

Invitations to a Boys' Stag-Party,

it should be suggested that the guests come in their old clothes, and not be late for the target-shooting. You must have some blow-guns and a target ready for them to use when they arrive.

Make the Target

of a large sheet of Manila paper. Outline the rings by placing the paper on the floor, driving a tack in the centre of the paper, and then using a piece of string with a loop at one end and a very short pencil at the other end, place the loop over the tack and fasten the pencil to the string. In this way make a number of circles, and number them from one to ten or fifteen, according to the number of guests you have invited to your stag-party.

When the target is finished lay it aside, and busy yourselves making darts for the blow-guns.   Take a number of

Carpet Tacks

and some bright-colored worsted ; tie the worsted string to the tack until the latter is covered, all but its point, then push all the ends of the strings back to the head of the tack and cut them off evenly, leaving them about a quarter of an inch long.

When one of these darts is shot through the blow-gun it will stick into anything it hits, unless the target be of stone or metal.

When the darts are all made lay them aside, with the blow-guns and the target, and go to the market and secure a basketful of an assortment of

FIGS. 280 AND 281

All the Large Vegetables

you can find—big turnips, the largest sweet potatoes, small squashes, field-beets, and compact cabbages. Some of the vegetables in this list may be out of season, but there will always be some that are in season.

Cut the top of each turnip, beet, potato, and squash, leaving a slanting or beveled edge to the lid (Fig. 280) ; then hollow out the vegetable until you have space enough to hold a fair-sized paper of candy.

Put the candy in oiled paper, place it in the hollow vegetable and fit the lid on the the top, where it can be secured
by using wooden toothpicks as tacks (Fig. 281). If this
work has been done with any sort of care, no one, not in
the secret, will suspect that it is not a common vegetable.

The Cabbage Bonbon Box

is made in the same manner, only in this case you must
carefully peel off the first covering of leaves from the head
of cabbage and then cut a hole for the bonbons, as in Fig.
282. After the candy is in place the leaves removed

READY FOR FILLING

SERVED.

FIGS. 282 and 283.

from the cabbage must be carefully replaced, and fastened
on with toothpicks, which are concealed by the surrounding leaves (Fig. 283).

When you have made one of these novel bonbon boxes
for each guest, you can begin to make

The Big Pie or Pudding

which is to grace the centre of the table. Buy a number of cheap toys, such as little china dolls (both black
and white), whistles, rattles, etc., and to each one you
attach a card with some comic verse or sentence written

on it; then you roll the toy up in a number of pieces of soft paper until the bundle assumes a ball-like form. The outside wrapper of each bundle should be of the brightest-

FIG. 284.—Attach a Bright Piece of Ribbon.

colored tissue-paper which can be found. After securely binding the bundles with twine attach a bright piece of tape or silk ribbon to each, as in Fig. 284.

When all the

Knick-knacks and Jokes

are bundled up, and the ribbons attached, place them in a large earthen dish or wooden bread-bowl, and arrange them so that the ribbon to each parcel hangs outside. Then fill the bowl with bran and pat into a rounded surface, as shown in Fig. 285.

The Ribbons Must be Loosely Knotted

at the sides, to keep them from harm, after which the surface of the "fake" cake is covered with a layer of wheat flour, to represent frosting, and the flour is ornamented with raisins, as in the illustration, while the top is decorated with a few sprigs of green or the ornaments from the top of a real cake, and the "fake" cake is then ready to serve.

Don't Disappoint the Boys.

While both the boys in knickerbockers and the boys in long-tailed coats like fun, neither the old nor the young boys enjoy being disappointed. You must, therefore, have some real pie, cake, and good things to serve, besides the make-believe cake, so as to keep all the guests good-humored.

The Shooting.

When all the lads have assembled and the target is in place, give one prepared tack and the blow-gun to one boy, and let him have a shot at the target, and keep account of the number he comes nearest to with the dart.

When all the boys have had their turn at firing a shot, and

The Numbers are All Recorded,

show them a list, with a penalty opposite each number; for instance, number one must wear two feathers in his hair; number two must have his face decorated with black circles; number three, face decorated with black stripes; number four, hair powdered white, with flour; number five, half face black, etc. Then tell them the list was made out by the Mad March Hare.

When All the Boys are Properly Decorated,

with blackened or whitened faces, coats wrong side out, etc., let them march to the table in the order of their numbers, and take the numbered seat which corresponds with the number they struck on the target. When the boys are seated the maid should bring in

Great Trays, Heaped with Raw Garden-Stuff.

This will cause a shout of surprise and disappointment; but after some lad has laboriously cut a great turnip in

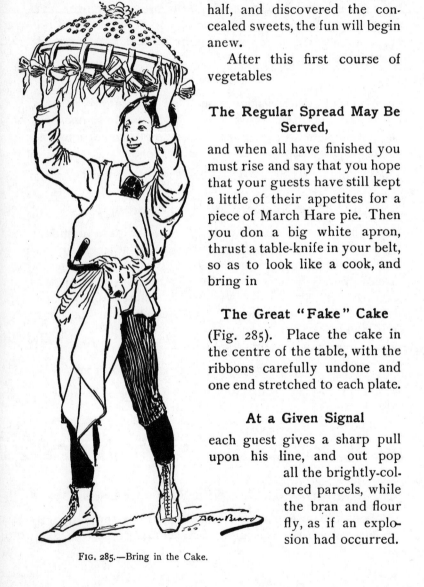

FIG. 285.—Bring in the Cake.

half, and discovered the concealed sweets, the fun will begin anew.

After this first course of vegetables

The Regular Spread May Be Served,

and when all have finished you must rise and say that you hope that your guests have still kept a little of their appetites for a piece of March Hare pie. Then you don a big white apron, thrust a table-knife in your belt, so as to look like a cook, and bring in

The Great "Fake" Cake

(Fig. 285). Place the cake in the centre of the table, with the ribbons carefully undone and one end stretched to each plate.

At a Given Signal

each guest gives a sharp pull upon his line, and out pop all the brightly-colored parcels, while the bran and flour fly, as if an explosion had occurred.

Feast of the Mad March Hare.

The success of this last act depends entirely upon the host. He must caution each boy not to gather in any of the slack of his ribbon, but only take a firm hold of the end and wait until the word is given to pull.

After the excitement and fun of demolishing the "fake" cake, then comes the fun of unrolling the bundles and reading the jokes attached to each trinket.

CHAPTER XXIV.

A WILD WEST SHOW IN THE HOUSE.

THERE are many boys to-day who have never seen an Indian, and while it is impossible for us all to view the real Wild West, it is not difficult for us to get up a little Wild West show of our own, at home.

Patterns Are Here Given,

which any intelligent boy can copy. The fields of the patterns given are divided into small squares, and the dividing lines are numbered and lettered along two sides of the pattern.

It is not hard to understand that, since every square, be it big or little, is exactly the same shape, by making the same number of larger squares you will have an enlarged field, similar to the one shown.

How to Reproduce the Patterns.

Place a clean piece of card-board on the table, and, with the aid of a straight-edged piece of board, rule a line close to the edge of the card-board and parallel to it.

By means of a two-foot measure, or tape-line, mark off with your pencil a point at each half-inch, to correspond with the numbered lines on the field (Fig. 286). Number the lines from one to thirty-three, as they are numbered in Fig. 286. Replace the straight-edged board along the line, take a large flat book (your geography will do), see that the

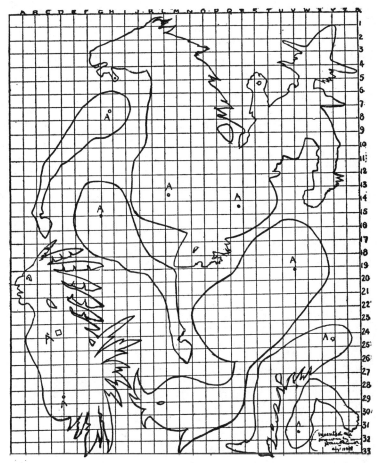

FIG. 286.—The Parts of Mounted Cowboy and Indian.

edge of the board is exactly parallel to the pencil line, and just far enough back of it to show the pencil dots, hold the board firmly in place, and slide the book along the edge of the board, until the edge of the book is exactly at the first pencil dot.

Rule the First Line

along the edge of the book, then move the book to the next

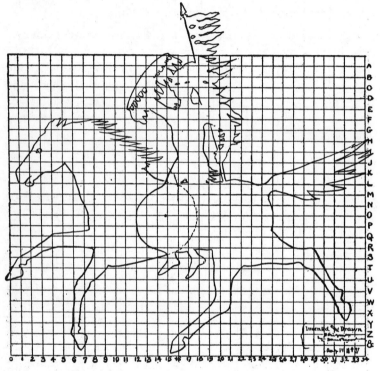

FIG. 287.—Mounted Indian.

dot and rule the line No. 1, then No. 2, and so on, until No. 33 is ruled.

Again Take Your Two-foot

rule or tape measure, and mark off by pencil dots the points for the lines at A, B, C, D, etc.; do the same on the line

No. 33, and with your board ruler connect with lines the two sets of dots, and you will have a field of squares exactly similar to the one in Fig. 286, only much larger.

Next Trace Out the Cowboy,

horse, and Indian, by drawing a line upon your enlarged field from point to point, as it is seen to cross the squares in the small pattern. In the pattern the Indian has but one leg and one arm, and the horse but one fore leg and one hind leg, but after these are cut out it is a simple matter to trace around them on card-board with a pencil, and thus supply all of the missing limbs.

After the Puppets Are Cut

out, punch holes with a darning-needle at the points marked A; these are the joints, and the spots where the parts are joined by a piece of string.

Make a Round Knot

in the end of a piece of string, so large that it will not pull through the needle-holes. Take the hind leg of the horse and thread the string through A, then through A upon the horse's hip, then through the hole in the other hind leg. Pull the string taut and, placing the puppet flat, tie a knot close to the leg (Fig. 289).

How it is Done.

To do this make a loose knot first, and with the forefinger of the left hand press the loop against the puppet while you slowly pull the free end taut (see Fig. 289). Tie it three or

four times, until the knot is too large to pull through the
needle-hole ; then cut off the end of the string.

Join all the limbs in the same manner, and the two parts
of the horse's body. The result will be a horse with a body
which will bend and legs which will move in a most natural
manner.

As the Audience

can see only the shadows, the joints will not be perceptible,
and the horse and rider can be made to take the most natural

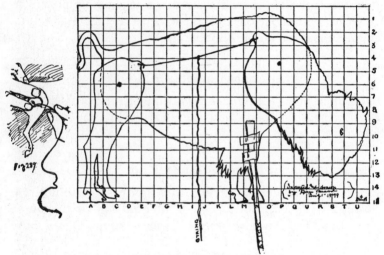

Figs. 288 and 289.—The Wild Buffalo.

poses. The silhouettes on the next page were traced from
a puppet made from this pattern.

For a Bridle

fasten a loop of string in the bit and the rider's hand. To
make the horse buck, fasten a piece of fine thread to his tail

A Bronco Buster.

and another piece to his head; then, by alternately pulling taut and allowing the thread to slacken, the horse will be found to jump, pitch, and buck, in a life-like and most approved Wild West manner.   Fig. 290 (the page illustration) shows a photograph made from the puppet here described, and Figs. 291, 292, 293, and 294 are positions assumed by that puppet, and traced directly from the paper horse and rider.

The Indian Horseman

(Fig. 287) shows how the body is joined; the dotted line indicates where the portion of the fore part of the body laps

under the hind part.   In Fig. 287 the legs are not jointed as in Fig. 286.   In drawing your pattern for this puppet make two fields of squares: one for the fore part and one for the hind part of the Indian and horse; and in Fig. 288 make three fields of squares, one for the hind legs, one for the body and one for the head.   Both of the last diagrams are drawn on one field to save space; but you can easily understand how to reproduce them.   For instance, in Fig. 287 make a field of squares from 0 to 18 for the fore part; make another field of squares from 12 to 34 for the hind quarters.

Make five or six duplicates of the Indian horseman;

make as many duplicates of the dancing Indians as may be required for your war-dance; do the same with

The Buffalo,

until you have a herd of them. Paste the flat end of a stick to the buffalo's leg and fasten a thread to the neck and hind

FIG. 295.

legs, as shown by Fig. 288. With the stick you move the bison along, and with the string you make him throw up his head and hind legs in a most amusing and comical manner.

A Piece of White Muslin,

stretched taut, with no wrinkles, will make your stage, and a light behind it will throw the shadows of your puppets on the cloth. The stage should be surrounded with heavy curtains, to prevent the operators from being seen, and the light behind the stage from illuminating the room in front. A bicycle lamp or an ordinary candle will answer for the light. A sheet of smooth Manila paper makes a better stage than the white cloth; it may be tacked upon a frame, or the bottom edge be tacked to a kitchen table and the top to a rod, suspended from the ceiling. The table should be on the audience side of the screen, so that the showmen may have room to move their puppet-sticks along the inside edge of the table, and keep the puppets close to the screen of paper. By changing the cowboy's hat to a soldier's cap or helmet, and putting a sword or gun in his hand, you can make as many cavalrymen from this pattern as you desire to have in the show.

CHAPTER XXV.

HOW TO HAVE A PANORAMA SHOW.

AFTER you have had a rollicking circus in the attic, and a roaring Wild West show in the basement, you can explain to your parents that a panorama is a show of a "highly moral" and most genteel character, and you may persuade them to allow you to have a panorama party in the dining-room.

A Good Panorama

is always a thing worth looking at, yet I promise you that there is more real enjoyment in making a panorama and exhibiting it, than there is in looking at twenty professiona' exhibitions.

The Subject

of the pictures must be your first thought. In their selection you have the widest possible range of choice, from the "Yankee in King Arthur's Court" to Roosevelt with the Rough Riders in Cuba, or from "The Pilgrim's Progress" to "Jack the Giant-killer," or "Mother Goose."

To those who have acquired the happy art of expressing their ideas with pencil and brush, the painting of an original panorama need not be explained; but the great majority of boys are unable to make pictures, either with pencil or with brush, and for them there remains still another method, which for beginners is equally, if not more effective.

With Paste-pot and Shears,

any boy, of ordinary ability, may make pictures galore by cutting the figures and even the backgrounds from illustrated papers, grouping and arranging them to suit himself, and pasting them neatly upon a long, strong strip or ribbon of paper, suited to winding and unrolling by means of two cylinders or rollers, as shown in Fig. 296.

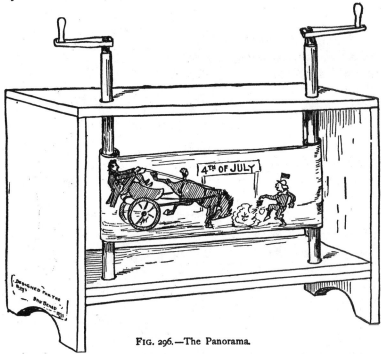

FIG. 296.—The Panorama.

Select Your Topic

first, then write out the number of illustrations you wish to make to tell the story; then hunt for a background here, a foreground there, and houses and people wherever they may be found. Paste the background on your strip of paper first, then the foreground, and next add the necessary number of people, vehicles, animals, and other objects.

YOU MAKE THE STAGE LIKE THIS

FIG. 297.

Colored Figures,

upon a white background, will be found to be most effective. Giants may be made by taking large-sized prints of men, clipping off their heads and replacing the latter with heads of smaller men. Dwarfs may be made by using the small

prints of men, and substituting big heads for the ones originally belonging to the figures.

Fig. 296 shows

The Works of the Panorama,

naked and unadorned.   But the machinery should be concealed, and for this purpose make a box, similar to the one
shown in Fig. 297, which is called the stage.   It is simply a
narrow box, as shown in Fig. 298, with drapery arranged
from the outer edges to a small
frame at the rear.   Fig. 297 is the
front of the finished stage; Fig.
298 is the rear of same, denuded of
its drapery.

FIG. 298.

Hiding in the cellar, basement,
attic, or woodshed, of almost every
house, are a lot of packing-cases,
but if from any cause these boxes
should be absent from their accus-
tomed places, you must go to your grocer for the material
for your stage.

Build a Narrow Box,

of about the proportions of Fig. 298, and make a frame of
four sticks for the back of the box; notch the cross-sticks
(Fig. 299) so that they will fit flush, or even, with the inside
surface of the two long pieces (Fig. 300).

Cut Some Dark Red Canton Flannel

into four pieces, to fit the four sides of your stage frame;
plait the ends, and tack each plait as the drapery is tacked
to the frame, as shown in Fig. 300.

After all four pieces of drapery are plaited and tacked fast, nail the frame to the back of the stage, as it is shown in

Fig. 300

THE CLOTH IS TACKED ON THE FRAME IN THIS WAY

FIGS. 299 and 300.

Fig. 298; then, one piece at a time, spread the edges of the cloth over the front edges of the box of the stage and tack them there, as in Fig. 297. This will give you a dark-colored stage frame with a small opening at the back end for the panorama to slide by, as the crank of the roller is turned by the showman behind the curtain.

Curtains must be arranged to hang down on each side of the stage and be pinned together above and below it.

The Stage

should rest upon a table, and be lighted by a row of small Christmas-tree candles, or common candles cut off and made short.

Whatever lights are used, care should be taken to place them so that there will be no danger from fire.

Of course it is not absolutely necessary to use candles for

Footlights.

Any sort of light which will illuminate the panorama without obstructing the view of the audience, will answer the purpose; but it is absolutely necessary to have no other

lights burning in the room while the panorama is being ex.
hibited. All the light must be centred upon the pictures.
Fig. 301 shows

How the Panorama Box

is built. There are two holes bored through the top board
and through the upper bottom board, but not through the
lower bottom board. A glance at the diagram will show you
that there are two bottom boards, fitting closely together.

Before putting the pano-
rama box together bore holes
in the top board, at equal
distances from the ends, and
as near the front edge as you
can conveniently bore them
without danger of splitting
the board. These holes are
for the rollers, and should be
of sufficient size to allow the

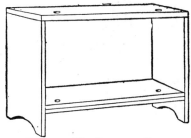

FIG. 301.—The Panorama Box.

rollers to revolve with little friction. In case you have no bit
or auger which will make large holes, Fig. 302 shows how
the difficulty may be overcome with a small bit, gimlet, or
red-hot poker, by boring a number of small holes in a circle
and then breaking out the centre-piece of wood; smooth-
ing the inside with a sharp knife. In order that the holes
in the bottom board shall be directly under those in the
top, nail the bottom board to the top board with three wire
nails, driving them in only just far enough to hold the
boards together while the holes are being bored, as shown
in Fig. 303. Since the

Top Board

fits over the side-pieces, and the bottom boards fit between

the side-pieces, it is evident that the bottom boards are
shorter than the top board by just the width of the two
side-pieces. Be careful to allow for this width at the ends,
when you nail the boards together, as shown in Fig. 303.

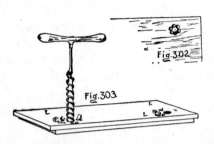

After the holes are
bored through the two
boards, nail the top board
and bottom boards in
place, as shown in Fig.
301.

You must, of course,
put the bottom board
with the holes in it, on top
of the bottom board without the holes. This will give two
sockets, in which to rest and turn the ends of the rollers.

Make the Rollers of Broomsticks,

if you can secure nothing better, but if you can find some
old window-shade rollers they will probably be an improvement on the broomsticks, as they have metal sockets in
which they will turn with much less friction than in the
wooden ones described above.

The rollers should both be of sufficient length to allow
a convenient amount of stick to protrude from the top of
the box, as is shown in Fig. 296.

A Crank or Windlass

handle, of some kind, is necessary to turn the rollers, and
Figs. 304 to 311 show how such handles may be made.

If you wish a comic panorama you have at your disposal
a vast amount of material. The gorgeously-colored comic

prints of to-day lend themselves readily to the process of picture-making with paste-pot and shears, and all sorts of funny combinations can be produced, which will delight the

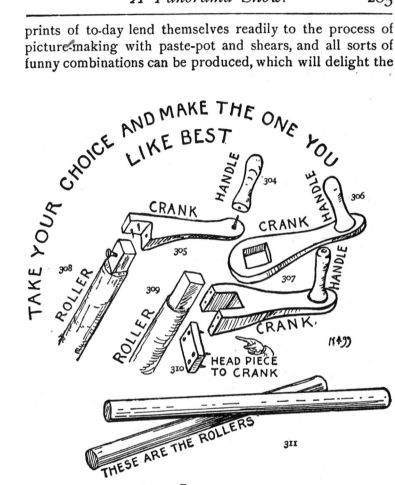

FIGS. 304-311.

audience, and, best of all, furnish indoor amusement and work for the reader when the weather is so boisterous, wet, and sloppy that there is no chance of fun out-of-doors, and there are many such days, between January and May, each year.

When all is done, paint some

Big Show-Bills,

to hang in the hallway, to be read and admired by the guests. Set the frame stage upon a small table, with the panorama box close against it; over the frame a small piece of dark cloth may be thrown, to be removed when the show begins.

The candles may be set upon a narrow strip of board, in front of the stage, and if you drive nails in groups of three, along the board, you will discover that the nails will hold the candles secure, as shown in the arrangement of the footlights in Fig. 312.

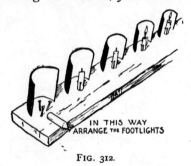

IN THIS WAY
ARRANGE THE FOOTLIGHTS

FIG. 312.

In front of each candle set

A Square Piece of Tin

bent to a curve, and with the concave side next to the candle, to act as a reflector, and the convex side next to the audience. The outsides should be painted dark red, to match the frame and conceal the light.

At the appointed time

Turn Out All the Lights

in the room, light the footlights, and remove the cloth from the box, displaying the first scene.

One boy should stand in front, as lecturer, and explain the different pictures, and another boy stand behind the curtain, winding up the paper as directed by the lecturer. The audience will have a good time, in proportion to the fun the lecturer puts in his talk, and all will enjoy the show **to**

THE END.

INDEX

INDEX

A

Ancient mariners, 5
Animals, kindness to, 33, 34
Ape, evolution of, 234
"Arab steed," how to make an, 254
Army, to make a pasteboard, 217
Artificial water, 206
Aviary, how to make a back-yard, 63
Axe, tree-top club-house built with, 10
Axles, car-wheel, 172

B

Bantam coops, 55
Beard, Frank, 224
Beard, Santa Claus's, 249
Bed, Daniel Boone cabin, 123; Lincoln, 124
Binders, to make water club-house foundation, 101
Birds, 63
Bonbon box, the cabbage, 265
Buffalo, to make a herd of, 276
Bugles, wooden, 141
Building material, house-boat, 150
Bumpers, house-boat, 155
Bunks, house-boat, 164
Burgoo, Kentucky, 107; ingredients of a, 109; how to cook a, 109
Burgoo master, 108, 109
Bridge of matches, 206
Bridle, to make a, 274

C

Cabin, how to build and furnish a Daniel Boone, 116; lumber for, 118; ground plan of 6 x 10, 119
Cabin, house-boat, 157; street-car used as, 168
Cage, to make a galvanized-wire netting, 39; receiving, 46
Cake, the "Fake," 266, 268
Camera, hunting with the, 20
Camp dress, women's, 133
Camping out. See Daniel Boone cabin, 116
Carp, 52
Carpet tacks as blow-gun darts, 264
Cars, back-yard switchback, 170
Catfish, 52
Centrepiece, house-boat, 151
Chalk talk, how to give a, 222
Chestnut wood for foundation posts, 75
Chickens, coops for, 54; need of shelter for, 54; material for coop, 56
Chimney, Daniel Boone cabin, 130; stick, 131; Santa Claus's, 238
Chipmonks, 19; how to trap, 26; food for, 26; wire cage for, 37
Circus, a home-made, 191; in the attic, 253
Clam-bake, the Rhode Island, 107
Clams, fresh-water, in confinement, 53

291